Why I am an Atheist
and
Other Writings

Bhagat Singh

THE MILKY WAY
PUBLICATIONS

ISBN: 978-81-991983-0-2

Publisher: The Milky Way Publications
Mumbai, Maharashtra

Phone: +91 916708046
WhatsApp: +91 9167080479
E-mail: themilkywaypublications@gmail.com

First Edition: 2025

Why I am an Atheist and writing
Bhagat Singh

Contents

Publisher's Note

"Why I Am an Atheist" is a powerful and introspective essay written by Indian revolutionary Bhagat Singh in 1930, while he was imprisoned in Lahore Central Jail. Singh, a prominent figure in India's struggle for independence, wrote this essay as a defense of his atheistic beliefs, particularly in response to criticism that his denial of God was rooted in vanity and arrogance rather than intellectual conviction.

In the essay, Singh addresses the idea that belief in God is essential for moral conduct, courage, and sacrifice. Many of his contemporaries believed that his steadfastness in the face of death must have been inspired by divine faith. Singh counters this assumption by explaining that his atheism was a deliberate and reasoned stance, not born of vanity or emotion. He acknowledges that earlier in his life, he was a believer and even performed religious rituals. However, his evolving political ideology and exposure to rationalist literature led him to question religious dogma and eventually reject the concept of God entirely.

Singh asserts that religious belief often stems from fear—particularly the fear of death and the unknown. He argues that religion serves as a psychological comfort rather than a rational explanation of the universe. For him, accepting God without evidence or logical basis is intellectually dishonest. Singh's atheism is not just a personal belief; it is rooted in a broader critique of organized religion and its role in justifying social inequalities and hindering progressive thought.

He writes that revolutionaries must cultivate a scientific temper and free themselves from all forms of superstition, including belief in divine justice or miracles. In this context, Singh's atheism is linked with his Marxist and socialist ideals. He believed that societal change must come from human effort and rational action, not divine intervention. Thus, he emphasizes the importance of reason, critical thinking, and the courage to face reality without resorting to supernatural explanations.

What makes Singh's essay particularly striking is its tone—confident, respectful, and deeply introspective. He never mocks religious believers but instead appeals to their reason. He acknowledges the emotional appeal of religion and the courage of religious martyrs but insists that his own path is driven by different convictions. He sees his atheism as a necessary extension of his revolutionary ideology—a way of breaking mental chains as much as political ones.

Bhagat Singh wrote this essay just a year before his execution, at the young age of 23. The clarity and maturity of thought displayed in the essay are remarkable, reflecting a deep commitment to intellectual freedom and personal integrity. His words continue to resonate with readers across generations, not just for their historical importance, but for their philosophical depth.

In conclusion, *Why I Am an Atheist* is not just a declaration of disbelief in God, but a manifesto for intellectual liberation. It challenges readers to think critically, question inherited beliefs, and seek truth through reason and evidence. Bhagat Singh's essay stands as a testament to his courage—not only in facing death, but in confronting the most fundamental questions of human existence with honesty and fearlessness.

Introduction

> "Sardar Bhagat Singh was a handsome young man, tall—5 ft. 10 inches, and well-built. He had a musical voice and could sing with emotion. One day, just after the sentences in the Assembly Bomb Case had been pronounced, his counsel, Mr. Asaf Ali with his wife, went to interview him. Bhagat Singh was locked up in a cell, and was in fetters. While they were approaching the cell, they heard a soft sweet voice singing in accompaniment of a twinkling metallic sound. Softly they approached, and lo[oked] ! They found Bhagat Singh the anarchist singing like a child and ringing his fetters in tune with the song."[1]

On October 7, 1930, Bhagat Singh and two others—Shivram Rajguru and Sukh Dev—were sentenced to be hanged by a Special Tribunal for the murder, in Lahore on December 17, 1928, of an Assistant Superintendent of Police, John Poyantz Saunders, as part of a conspiracy to wage war against the government of India under British rule. It was a tragic case of mistaken identity. They had intended to kill the Superintendent of Police, J.A. Scott, who, they believed, had struck the blows on Lala Lajpat Rai during a procession in Lahore on October 30, 1928.

The entire country was exercised over the Simon Commission which was touring India as part of its remit to recommend the next instalment of constitutional reforms. The British Government did not appoint on the Commission a single Indian member which was a cause of great concern for the Indian public.

Some of Lahore's most distinguished public figures met outside Mochi Gate before marching in the fateful procession. This meeting was to coincide with the Simon Commission's arrival in Lahore that day and was only the last of a series of meetings. On October 30 agitated Scott turned on the

1. From *Sardar Bhagat Singh* by Jatinder Sanyal, published in May 1931.

demonstrators without any provocation and led the police assault. Lajpat Rai was his special target. He received injuries on the chest and elsewhere. On November 17, Lajpat Rai, the 'Punjab Kesri' took his last breath. The country was stunned as news of the death spread and so was Bhagat Singh who along with his comrades decided to avenge Lala's death by killing Scott. Only hours after the deed did he realise that it was not Scott but his junior whom he and his colleague Rajguru had killed.

On April 8, 1929, Bhagat Singh and Batukeshwar Dutt each threw a bomb in the chamber of the Central Legislative, while it was in session, and scattered leaflets to express the disagreement with the ordinance of Defense of Indian Act that was to be formulated. The intention was not to kill but to deliver a message which is why Bhagat Singh fired two unaimed shots from the pistol. Six members of the Assembly were injured. They disdained escape and readily gave themselves up.

In jail, he witnessed discrimination between the European and Indian prisoners and led a hunger strike to protest against this. They demanded equality in food standards, clothing, etc for "political prisoners". After a month's strike, the British were forced to agree to their demands.

The pistol seized from him in the Assembly was afterwards proved to have been used in the Saunders' murder. And soon Bhagat Singh, Sukhdev and Rajguru were convicted of assassinating John Saunders and exploding the bomb at the Legislative Assembly Hall and the order of death sentence, to be executed on 24th March 1931 was passed. But the schedule was preponed and they were hanged on March 23, 1931 at 7:30 PM in the Lahore jail.

Bhagat Singh remains an unparalleled icon in the history of India's freedom struggle. Singh was 23 when he forfeited his life for his motherland. His and his comrades' martyrdom remains a significant point in history. Jawaharlal Nehru in his autobiography writes about Singh:

> "He became a symbol [...] and within a few months each town and village of the Punjab, and to a lesser extent in the rest of northern India, resounded with his name. Innumerable songs grew up about him, and the popularity that the man achieved was something amazing."

His popularity back then knew no bounds and this remains true even today. This makes us often wonder how was it possible for a young lad to sacrifice his life for his nation. What was he thinking? Was it just a fluke? Or was he manipulated? And most importantly, why is he so popular?

The primary enabling factor for Bhagat to answer his nation's call was probably his ancestral fervour to stand against the British. Bhagat Singh was born on September 27, 1907 in a celebrated Sikh family in village Banga in the Lyallpur district of the Punjab state under British rule. He was the second of seven children—four sons, and three daughters—born to Vidyavati and her husband Kishan Singh Sandhu. His ancestors were Khalsa Sardars who helped in the spread of the Sikh kingdom under Maharaja Ranjit Singh.

Bhagat Singh's grandfather, Sardar Arjun Singh was a respected landlord. He was a man of strong feelings for social reforms. The injustice perpetrated by the British Raj was not something he was able to overlook and he fervently opposed the British rule in India. When his extended family was joining hands with the British and benefitted from it, he chose a path which inevitably led to being in the bad books of the British and ultimately to poverty. Yet, he openly advocated for India's freedom. In his family, he often told stories of his own grandfather, Fateh Singh who stood against the British during the first struggle for independence in 1857. Fateh Singh had helped Muslim tenants to get land rights and later unlike other big land owners, refused an offer to get more land by entering into a deal with the British. Fateh Singh believed in the teaching of Guru Gobind who urged people to stand with struggle for justice. Arjun Singh carried this tradition further and encouraged his three sons to join the freedom struggle and reform movements.

Bhagta's grandfather was a man of action and many of his qualities could be found in Bhagat too. He was a liberalist who believed that emancipation of the country will only come about when each downtrodden group in the country is empowered. He always urged himself and his family to work toward this goal. He maintained good relationships with farm workers and took care of their needs. He also provided free medicare to the needy. At a time when the education of girls was frowned upon, he gave the name 'Vidyawati' to his eldest daughter-in-law (Bhagat Singh's mother). He encouraged his daughters-in-law to carry out various constructive activities to help villagers such as educating girls and providing a helping hand to the needy. He along with his wife and other family members supported the upbringing of about 22 orphan children, most of whom later contributed to the freedom movement with utmost devotion.

Arjun Singh was so full of nationalist spirit that at 80 years old, he still took a keen interest in the proceedings of the Lahore Conspiracy Case. And matching his spirit was Bhagat Singh's grandmother, Jai Kaur. Her efforts were equally motivated as her husband in emancipating the nation and uplifting its people. She was a gutsy lady who once saved Sufi Amba Prasad, one of the pioneer nationalists of India. She raised three sons, Sardar Kishen Singh, Sardar Ajit Singh and Sardar Swaran Singh who came to be known throughout the country for their sincere service to the country.

On the day Bhagat Singh was born, all three brothers, Bhagat's father and uncles— Kishen Singh, Ajit Singh and Swaran Singh— were in jail for anti-British activities. In fact, Swaran Singh died the very same year in jail. Ajit Singhworked closely with Lala Lajpat Rai. Bhagat Singh grew up on stories of the exploits of his uncles and his father. The Ghadar movement left a deep imprint on his mind. Kartar Singh Sarabha, hanged when he was only nineteen after conviction in the first Lahore Conspiracy case, became his hero.The massacre at Jallianwalla Bagh on Aprill3, 1919 was another incident that had a great impression on 12 years old Bhagat Singh's mind. He went to Amritsar and brought back the blood-soaked soil making a promise to avenge them and drive the British out of India.

Though it was customary for the Sikhs to join the Khalsa High School, Kishen Singh had no liking for the School owing to the loyalist tendencies of its authorities. So Bhagat Singh joined the D. A. V. School in Lahore, an Arya Samajist school. Bhagat Singh left the D.A.V. School in 1921 and joined the National College, started by Lala Lajpat Rai and Sufi Amba Prasad where he met his Sukh Dev, Bhagwati Charan Vohra, and Yash Pal. Also, after the failure of the non-cooperation movement in 1921, Bhagat's belief in non-violence as a means to achieve independence weakened and he resorted to siding with revolutionary nationalism. Arevolutionary sect in Punjabknown as Babbar Akalis came up during this time and Kishen Singh is known to have funded the sect.

Bhagat Singh then went to Kanpur where Ganesh Shankar Vidyarthi gave him a job at his press. In the next six months he spent in Kanpur, he learnt a lot. Vidyarthi was a member of the All India Congress Committee. His house was a hub for political activists. It is here that Bhagat met Batukeshwar Dutt and Chandrashekhar Azad, and formally joined the Hindustan Republican Association. The Association was formed in 1923 with the aim to attain

India's freedom with armed revolution. Funds were raised for its functioning, among other things by committing dacoities. Three went unnoticed. The fourth was near the Kakori railway station near Lucknow on August 9, 1925. The accused were punished severely, some hanged, some imprisoned for life. These savage sentences weakened the Association. Bhagat Singh returned to Lahore and in March 1926, he formed the Naujawan Bharat Sabha along with Sukh Dev, Bhagwati Charan Vohra and Ram Krishan which took up the unfulfilled mission of the Hindustan Republican Association. Singh aimed to encourage revolution against British rule by rallying the peasants and workers.

His motivation and unparalleled determination to fight for his cause not only came from the people around him but also through books. Singh was an ardent reader. He was highly inspired by the ideas of Lenin and Karl Marx and believed in socialism. His exposure to world literature was immense. Shiv Verma, one of his comrades in jail, wrote:

> "We had easy access to books in the jail since the day one and the atmosphere was quite congenial for study and exchange of ideas... but Bhagat Singh's arrival made this much more lively...Though we all had a passion for reading, but Bhagat Singh was a class by himself. Despite his soft corner for socialism, he was passionate about fiction as well, particularly with political and economic themes. Dickens, Upton Sinclair, Hall Cane, Victor Hugo, Gorky and Oscar Wilde were among his favourites."

It was due to this exposure, he was not just a raw nationalist. He was a thinker. He was not just a patriot with a passionate commitment to his nation, he was a visionary, with a pluralist and egalitarian perception of independent India.He was committed to *Inquilab* (revolution) but it was not merely a political revolution he aimed at. He wanted a social revolution to break the age-old discriminatory practice. He also wrote extensively on issues of caste, communalism and conditions of the working class and peasantry. The profundity of his ideas isvisible in his regular columns in *Kirti*, *Arjun*, *Pratap* and other magazines and papers.Justtwenty days before his martyrdom on 3 March 1931, Bhagat Singh sent out an explicit message to the youth saying:

> ". . . the struggle in India would continue so long as a handful of exploiters go on exploiting the labour of the common peoplefor

> their own ends. It matters little whether these exploiters are purely British capitalists, or British and Indians in alliance,or even purely Indians."

It is these ideas, this vision that makes him an inspirational figure, not just for the youth of those times but even today. He left behind an intellectual legacy, a huge collection of political and social writings on burning issues of contemporary importance like caste, religion, communalism, language, and politics.

The writings collected in this book are written by Bhagat Singh on various occasions which reflect his thought and personality. These writings not only describe his political beliefs but also his views on social, religious and philosophical matters. Prompt, direct and concerned—his writings unabashedly reflect the troubles of revolutionaries, the attitude of the colonial rulers and the situation of the Indian socio-political milieu. These writings hold importance not only from a historical point of view but also hold a mirror for our present generation on various issues of contemporary importance.

Bhagat Singh, standing 3rd right, in a 1923 photo of National College Lahore Dramatics Club. (Source: The Indian Express)

Bhagat Singh's ancestral house at Khatkar Kalan.

Bhagat Singh at age 12.

1

The Problem of Punjab's Language and Script

The Punjab Hindi Sahitya Sammelan,in 1923, organised an essay competition on the topic 'The Problem of Punjab's Language and Script'. Bhagat Singh wrote this articlefor that competition. Bhagat Singh got a prize of Rs. 50 for this article. Subsequently, it was published in *Hindi Sandesh* on February 28, 1933.

"An acquaintance of the literature of a society or a country is of prime importance for the understanding of that society or country, because the consciousness of the soul of a society or country, because the consciousness of the soul of a society gets reflected in its literature also." History is witness to the authenticity of the above statement. Countries have followed the direction determined by the flow of their literature. Every nation needs literature of high quality for its own uplift. As literature of a country attains new heights, the country also develops. Patriots — be they merely social reformers or political leaders — pay highest attention to the literature of their country. If they do not create new literature to meet the requirements of the contemporary issues and situations, all of their efforts will fail and their work will prove unstable.

Perhaps Garibaldi could not have succeeded in mobilising the army with such ease if Mazzini had not invested his thirty years in his mission of cultural and literary renaissance. The revival of Irish language was attempted with the same enthusiasm along with the renaissance in Ireland. The rulers so much wanted to suppress their language for the ultimate suppression of the Irish people that even kids were punished for the crime of keeping a few verses in Gaelic. The French revolution would have been impossible without the literature of Rousseau and Voltaire. Had Tolstoy, Karl Marx and Maxim Gorky not invested years of their lives in the creation of a new literature, the

Russian Revolution would not have taken place, leave alone the propagation and practice of communism.

The same applies to the social and religious reformers. Kabir's ideas have a stable impact because of his literature. Till date, the sweetness and sensitivity of his poems prove captivating to the people.

Exactly the same can be said about Guru Nanak Devji, When the Sikh Gurus started establishing their new order along with the preaching of their beliefs, they felt the need of a new literature and this inspired Guru Angad Devji to evolve the Gurumukhi script. Centuries of continuous warfare and Muslim invasions had dried up the literature of Punjab. The Hindi language was at the verge of extinction. He adopted the Kashmiri script in his search for an Indian language. Later the Adi Granth was compiled by Guru Arjun Devji and Bhai Gurudasji. They took a far-reaching and useful step in this act of creating their own script and literature to perpetuate their beliefs.

Afterwards, as situations changed, the flow of literature also changed. The ceaseless sacrifices and sufferings of the Gurus changed the situation. Whereas we find devotion and self-oblivion in the preaching of the first Guru, and experience a sense of self-effacement in the following couplet:

Nanak nanhe ho rahe, jaisi nanhi doob.
Aur ghas jari jaat hai, doob khoob ki khoob

(Nanak asks all to be as humble and insignificant as the doob grass. While all other grasses are burnt down, doob continues to flourish.)

We find a sense of fellow-feeling and helpfulness for the oppressed in the preaching of Guru Shri Teg Bahadurji:

Baanhi jinhan di pakadiye, sir dijiye baanhi na chhodye,
Guru Teg Bahadur bolya, dharati pai dharam na chodye.

(Whomsoever you provide protection, you should be prepared to sacrifice yourself but not that protection. Guru Teg Bahadur asks you not to forsake your religion on this earth.)

After his sacrifice, suddenly, we sense a warrior spirit in the preaching of Guru Gobind Singhji. When he realised that a mere spiritual devotion could not do anything, he started Chandi worship and turned Sikh community into a community of worshippers and warriors by synthesising spiritualism and fighting. We find in his poems (literature) a new spirit. He writes:

Je tohi prem khelan da chav, sir dhar tali gali mori aav,
Je it maarag pair dharijai, sir dijai kaan no dijai.

(If you are interested in playing the game of love, put your head on your palm and then only enter my lane. In case you put your feet on this path don't fall back, even if you have to loose your life.) And then:

Soora so pahchaniye, je lade deen ke het,
Purja-purja kat mare, kabhu na chhade khet.

(Only he is brave who fights for the cause of the poor. He may be cut into pieces and may be killed, but he should not leave the field.)

And then suddenly, the sword-worship starts.

Carrying the same spirit Baba Banda and others fought Muslim ruler ceaselessly. We find later that when Sikhs are reduced to mere groups of anarchists, declared outlaws, and were continuously compelled to be confined to the forests, no new literature could be created. They had a warrior spirit, a sense of courage and sacrifice and a spirit to continue their war against Muslim rulers, but they could not chalk out their future beyond this . This explains why these warrior groups fought among themselves. It is here that their lack of contemporary spirit worries us. If a warrior and shrewd ruler like Ranjit Singh had not emerged afterwards, Sikhs would have gone down bereft of any high ideal or spirit to have mobilised them.

Along with all this, one more point deserves attention. All the Sanskrit literature, put together, failed to revive the Hindu society; new literature had to be written in a contemporary modern language. Till date, we feel only the effect which was created by that literature of contemporary spirit. Even for a person of proper education and comprehension, the hymns of unintelligible Sanskrit and ayat (verses) of classical Arabic cannot be as enthusing as is possible by the simple statements in a simple language.

A short history of Punjabi language and literature is sketched out above. Now we turn to our times. Swami Vivekananda in Bengal and Swami Ramtirtha in Punjab were born approximately at the same time. Both were 'great' in the same sense. Both got fame for establishing Indian metaphysics abroad. Swami Vivekanand's mission became a permanent institution in

Bengal while Punjab misses a memorial to Swami Ramtirtha. In spite of having significant differences in their thinking, we find strong similarities at the roots. Whereas Swami Vivekananda was preaching Karma Yoga, Swami Ramtirtha was singing in blissfulness:

Ham rukhe tukade khayenge,
Bharat par ware jayenge,
Hum sukhe chane chabayenge,
Bharat ki baat banyenge,
Ham nange umar bitayenge,
Bharat par jaan mitayenge.

(We shall subsist on crumbs but sacrifice ourselves for Bharat. We shall eat the most ordinary food, but work for our country. We shall go naked the whole life, but offer our lives for Bharat.)

Several times, he wept while seeing the setting sun in America, and said: "Now you are rising in my beloved country. Drop my tears like dew-drops over beautiful water-fed fields of India." Such a great devotee of the country and God was born in our province and , if we do not have even a single memorial to him, what else could explain that, except our literary backwardness?)

This we feel at every step. Many great men born in Punjab, who are comparable to Shri Devendra Thakur and Keshav Chandra Sen of Bengal, but we did not respect them and easily forgot them after their deaths—for example, guru Gyan Singhji, etc. We find only one reason on bottom, and that is the total lack of literacy interest and awakening, The truth is that no country or community can progress without its literature. But language is the primary need of literature and this is absent in Punjab. In spite of releasing this handicap for long, the question of language has still remained unresolved. The main reason behind this is the unfortunate communalisation of language in our province, in other provinces, we find that Muslims have fully adopted their provincial languages. In the literary world of Bengal. Poet Nazrul-Islam is a shining star. Latif Hussain 'Natwar' is prominent among the Hindi poets. The same is true of Gujrat also. But Punjab is unfortunate. Here, even Hindus and Sikhs are not united, leave the Muslims alone.

Punjab should have been the language of Punjab, like other provinces, but since this has not happened, as this question is a spontaneous question, Muslims have adopted Urdu. Muslims totally lack Indianness, therefore they want to propagate Arabic script and Persian language. While failing to understand the importance of Indianness in the whole of India, they fail to understand the importance of one language, which could only be Hindi. That is why they keep repeating the demand for Urdu like a parrot and take an isolated position.

Then comes the turn of the Sikhs. Their whole literature is in the Gurumukhi script. Hindi is very much there as a component, but Punjabi constitutes the main component. Therefore, the Sikhs adopted Punjabi written in Gurmukhi as their language. They could not leave that at any cost. They embraced that by making it a communal language.

The Arya Samaj emerged on the other side. Swami Dayanand propagated the feeling for the spread of Hindi throughout Bharatvarsha. Hindi became a religious component of the Arya Samaj movement. These religious attachments benefited the language in one way. That is , while Sikh staunchness secured Punjabi, the insistence of Arya Samajists helped Hindi secure a place of its own.

In the early days of Arya Samaj movement, the Sikhs and Arya Samajists used to have religious gathering at the same place. At that time they had no feelings of being different, but afterwards, a few sentences of Satyartha Prakash caused malice and mutual hatred. The Sikhs, swept in the same stream, started hating even Hindi as well. Other did not take even notice of it.

Afterwards, it is said, a Samaji leader, Mahatma Hansraj Ji held consultations with many leaders and proposed that if they accept the Hindi script, he would get the Punjabi language in Hindi script, and he would get the Punjabi language in Hindi script recognised in the University. But they could not understand the importance of this proposal because of their narrow-mindedness and absence of literary awareness. At this moment, three views prevail in Punjab. Firstly, there is strong attachment for urdu among the Muslims; secondly, for Hindi among Arya Samajis and certain other Hindus; and thirdly, for Punjabi.

It will not be important here to deal with all the languages one by one. First of all, we shall consider the Muslims view. They are staunch supporters of Urdu. At the present time, this language is dominant in Punjab. This is also the language of the court. Then some Muslims say that Urdu scripts saves space. This may be quite right, but the most important question before us at this juncture is to make India a unified nation, but this cannot be done all at once. For this we have to move step by step. If we cannot adopt one language for the whole of India at the moment, we should at least adopt one script. The urdu script cannot be called a perfect one and the most important point is that it is based on the Persian language. The flights of imagination of urdu poets—even if they are Hindi (Indian)—reach the saaqis (bar-maids) of Persia and date palms of the Arbs countries. Kazi Nazrul-Islam's poems refer to Dhurjate, Vishwamitra and Durvasa quite frequently, but our Punjabi Hindi-Urdu poets could not even think of them. Is it not a matter which makes one sad? Their ignorance of Indianness and Indian literature is the main reason of this. When they cannot imbibe Indianness, how can their literature make us Indian? Students confined to the study of Urdu cannot attain knowledge of the classical literature of India. It is not that these texts cannot be translated into a literary language like Urdu, but it will be useful only to a Persian in his pursuit of Indian literature.

It will Suffice to say in support of the above statement that when simple words like Arya and Swarajya are written as 'Ariya' and 'Swarajia', what will happen to the deep metaphysical topics? Only a few days back, a government translator, using the urdu script, mistook sage Nachiketa as 'Neechi Kutia' which can be translated as a 'bitch of low origin', while translating an Urdu book Qaumen kis Tarah Zinda Rah Sakti Hain (How nationalities can survive) by Lala Hardayalji, M.A. It was neither Lalaji's fault nor the translator. It was only a shortcoming of the Urdu script and the dissimilarity between Urdu and Hindi languages and literature.

Indian languages and script prevail in the rest of India. In such a situation, should we get absolutely isolated from India point is that, among Muslim writers, the staunch supporters of Urdu write highly Persianised Urdu. The Muslim newspapers like Zamindar and Siyasat have strong Arabic influence which is quite incomprehensible to common people. How can this be propagated in such a situation? We wish our Muslim brothers, while sticking to their religion, think of Indianising themselves like Kamal the Turk. India's salvation is possible only that way. Instead of making language a communal question, we should adopt a wide perspective.

We will now return to the problem of Hindi and Punjabi. Many idealists entertain a vision of the world turned into one single nation, one global nation. This ideal is beautiful and one should keep it before oneself. But this cannot be achieved today; all of our steps, all of our efforts should be directed towards enhancement of happiness by uniting all nationalities, countries and nations into one strong bond. Before that, we have to realise that ideal in our own country. We have to adopt one language, one script, one literature, one ideal and one nation, but the adoption of a single language precedes all the other unities, so they we can communicate with and comprehend each other. A Punjabi and a Madrasi must not sit together mute at a gathering, but try to communicate their ideas and emotions, and this should be done in our own language, Hindi, rather than in an alien language like English. Even this ideal will take years to be realised. First of all, we should create literary awareness in this endeavor, not among a few but in the masses. The people's own language is essential for creating literary awareness among the people. On the basis of this logic, we say that you can succeed in Punjab only in Punjabi language.

Till now, Punjabi has not been able to become a literary language of the central Punjab. It is written in the Gurmukhi script and is now Known as Punjabi. It is neither widely prevalent nor has any literature or scientific significance. It was left unattended earlier, but even now the deficiency of its script disturbs those who are now attending to it. All the words, cannot end without the sound 'a' and its inability to write compound letter; even the word 'Poorna' (complete) cannot be written. This script is thus even more incomplete than Urdu, but when we already have a scientific and perfect Hindi script, what is there to feel hesitant about adopting it? The Gurmukhi script is only distorted form of the Hindi script. Right from the start all the rules are same, then, how much will we be benefited by our immediate switch over to this. The Punjabi language will start developing immediately by adopting this perfect script. And there is no problem in the propagation of it. Hindu women of Punjab already know this script. The DAV school and Sanatan Dharma schools teach only in Hindi, what could be the problem in such a situation? We shall plead with the supporters of Hindi that, ultimately and certainly, only Hindi will be the language of the whole Bharat, but it will be more convenient to propagate it from now on. Punjabi will become like Hindi by adopting the script and then all the differences will disappear; and it is desirable, too that common people could be educated which is possible only through our own language in our own script. See this Punjabi poem:

O rahiya rahe jandya, sun ja gall meri
Sir to pag tere balait di, ihnun fuk muatara la.

(O passer by, listen to me. Burn that foreign turban which thou art wearing on thy head, And take to 'Muatara'.)

Even beautiful Hindi poems cannot cast an impression comparable to this, as they have not yet made a place right in the hearts of the people. They still seem somewhat alien. It is so because Hindi is based on Sanskrit. And the Punjab has gone farther away from that. Persian has maintained its dominance in Punjab to a large extent. For example, a collection of things become 'cheezan' here instead of 'cheezain'. This principle prevails throughout. What is being emphasised here is that Hindi is still far from Punjabi heart in spite of being close to Punjabi; of course, Punjabi will come closer to Hindi when it will adopt the Hindi script attempt creating its literature.

By now almost every major issue has been discussed here. Only one thing now remains to be said. Many people argue that the Punjabi language lacks sweetness, beauty and emotions. This is absolutely baseless. Only recently the sweetness, beauty and emotions. This is absolutely baseless. Only recently the sweetness, beauty and emotions of this song hypnotised Kavindra Ravindra:

Lachhiye, jitthe tu pani doliya,
Utthe ug paye sandal de boote.

(O Lachhi, where you split water at that place sandlewood trees have sprouted.)

Many more examples could be cited. Is the following couplet even the least inferior to the poems of any other language?

Pipal de pattya ve kehi khadkhad layee ae,
Patte jhade purane hun rut navayan di aayee ae.

(Pipal leaves, why are you making noise? The old leaves have fallen and the season for new leaves has come.)

And when Punjab is sitting alone or in a group, will any other language move them to the extent these lines of Gauhar can:

Lam lakkhan to karoran de shah vekhe
Na musafiran koi udhar dende,
Dine raatin de kuch dere,
Na unhan gulan di vasana te
Bhauren bahande gulan di vasana te

Na sappan de muhan te koi pyar denda,
Gauhar same salook han jyuadya de
Moyan giyan un tar koi visar denda.

(I have seen armies of lakhs of millionaires. No one gives loan to the passers-by who never stay, never reside in one place. No one trusts them. Black beetles sit on flowers because of their smell. No one gives love to the hoods of the snakes. O Gauhar, good behaviour and welcome is for those who are alive, but everyone says good-bye at the time of death.)

Jeev jyudiyan nu kyon marna ae
Jekar nahintu moyan nn jiaun joga,
Ghar aaye sawali nu kyon ghurna ae
Jekar nahin tu hatthin khair joga;
Mile dilan naun kayaker todna ae
Mile dilan tu bichhadyan nu milaun joga,
Gauhar barhiya rakh band khaane
Jekar nahin tu nekiyan kumaun joga.

(Why kill living beings when you are not able to bring the dead back to life? Why do you stare at the beggar who has come to your door when you are not able to give him something? Why break the union of hearts if you are not able to reunite hearts that are separated? O Gauhar, if you cannot do go to others, then keep your good food and room closed.)

And nowadays brilliant poets like Dard, Mastana, Dewana are enriching the Punjabi's poetry.

It is a pity that such a sweet, such a captivating language has not been adopted even by the Punjabis themselves. They still refuse; and this is the crux of the problem. Everyone backs his arguments on the basis of religious convictions. The only problem concerning the language and script of Punjab is to remove this obstruction, but the hope lies in the increasing literary awareness among the sikhs. Hindu also have it. Why not at all well-meaning people decide by mutual deliberations? This is the only way to arrive at a solution. The question can be attended to by renouncing religious considerations. It should be attempted accordingly and the recognition of Punjabi language of a journal like Prem of Amritsar. This way the problem is resolved. After the elimination of this irritant, Punjab will have such beautiful and 'quality' literature that it will also be counted among the good language of India.

2

Problem of Untouchability

Bhagat Singh wrote this wonderful piece at the age of 16 in June 1923. It was later published in *Kriti* in 1928.

Our country is in a trulydirestate; most bizarre inquiries are madehere, the foremost involvingthe untouchables, who makeup 6 crores of 30 crores population in our country.

For example:-

Would contact with an untouchable mean defilement of an upper caste? Would not the gods in the temples, get angry at the entry of untouchables there? Would not the drinking water of a well get polluted if the untouchables drew their water from the same well? That these questions are being asked in the twentieth century, is a matter that puts us to shame.

We Indians boast of our spiritualism, but then, we avoid accepting every human being as a fellow being just like ourselves. Western people on the other hand, who carry a reputation of being money minded, had unequivocally affirmed their faith in the principle of equality. This they did during the revolutions in America and France and above all in Russia, which these daysis committed to the extension of this principle to all aspects of life and to the eradicationof discrimination in any form whatsoever, thereby fulfilling the ideals of May Day declaration. But we Indians, who never tire of boasting about our gods and godliness are, yet seriously debating whether to allow the untouchables to wear the sacred thread or the *janeu* and whether the untouchables be permitted to read Vedas / Shastras. We often complain about our mistreatment in other countries, and especially when we are maltreated by the whites, do we have any moral right to voice such disapproval?

In 1926, a Sindhi Muslim gentleman, Mr. Noor Mohd member of Bombay Legislative Council aptly remarked:- "If the Hindu society refuses to allow other human beings, fellow creatures at that, to attend public schools, and if .... The president of the local board representing so many lakh of people, in his house, refuses to allow his fellows and brothers, the elementary human right of having water to drink, what right have they to ask for more rights from the bureaucracy? Before we accuse the people coming from other lands, we should see how people... how can we ask for greater political rights when (we ourselves) deny elementary rights of human beings?

How true! But since this had been said by a Muslim, Hindus lost no time in declaring that the Muslim's real intention was to convert the untouchables to Islam and thus assimilate them into their own brotherhood. But then, it led to an open admission of the harsh truth–that if you (the Hindus) treat them worse than your cattle, they shall desert you and join the fold of other religions where they hope to enjoy more rights, where they are treated as fellow beings.

Would it not then be futile to accusethe Christians and Muslims, that they were undermining Hinduism?

How fair and true! Yet the Hindus shudderin anger on hearing this plain truth. In any case, it had jolted Hindus from their complacency in the matter. Orthodox Brahmins also began re-thinking it, also joined by some self-proclaimed reformers. At Patna, a gala Hindu meet was held. Lala Lajpat Rai, known for his longstanding sympathy for the untouchables was presiding. A lot of hot arguments were exchanged as to whether the untouchables are eligible to wear the sacred thread, the *janeu*? May they read Vedas / Shastras? Several social reformers lost their temper but Lala ji was able to persuade them to compromise on these two matters and thereby saved the prestige of Hindu religion; otherwise, what would have been the consequences?

Just imagine how shameful! Even a dog can sit in our lap, it can also move freely in our kitchens but if a fellow human touches you, your dharma isjeopardised. So much so, even a reputed social reformer like Pandit Malviya ji, known for his soft corner for the untouchables, first agrees to be publicly garlanded by a sweeper, but then later considershimself to be polluted till he bathes and washes those clothes. How ironical! In the temples meant for worshipping God, who lives in us all, a poor man enters itonce, it gets defiled and God gets annoyed. When this is the state of affairs within the Hindu fold, do we look good fighting for equality from the outsiders? Above all, this kind of approach that we have to the question amounts to an ingratitude of the degree; those who provide us with the comforts by doing menial jobs for us, we shun them. We could worship even animals, but would not tolerate fellow humans sitting beside us.

This is a burningissue of debate these days, the poor creatures are getting special attention in this way. In the context of our advance towards national liberation, the problem of communal representation (seats in the legislatures allotted in proportion to Hindu/ Sikh/ Muslim population) may not have been beneficial in any other manner but atleast Hindu / Muslim / Sikhs are all striving hard to maximize their own respective quota of seats by attracting the maximum number of untouchables to their own respective folds. Accordingly, Muslims started by providing them equal rights after converting them to Islam.

This naturally pains the Hindus. Bitterness mounted, and riots broke out as well. By and by Sikhs, too woke up lest they be left behind in this race. They too started administering Amrit; tension mounted between Sikhs and Hindus over the removal of *janeu* or hair shaving. All in all, all three are trying to surpass the others, causing widespread disturbances. Christians sitting on the fence are quietly consolidating their hold. Be as it may, this turmoil is certainly helping us to move towards the weakening of the hold of untouchability.

As for themselves, when they learnt that all this great mayhem was over them and all were trying to gain benefits for themselveson their account, they also thought, "Why should we not organize on our own?" It is not certain whether the government is behind the execution of this thought or if they are doing it on their own but it is for sure that this trend is being fully backed up by official quarters. "Adi Dharam Mandal" and the likes are the outcome of this trend.

Here, the basic question arises, what is the most effective way to solve this problem? The answer is quite clear; above all, it needs to be settled for good, that all humans are equal without distinctions of birth or vocation. In other words,because someone is born into a poor sweepers' family, that is why he shall continue cleaning toilets all his life and thus be deprived of all chances of progress in life, all this is baloney. Historically speaking, when our Aryan ancestors nurtured these practices of discrimination towards these strata of society, shunning all human contact with them by tagging them as menials and assigning all the degrading jobs to them, they also, naturally started worrying about a revolt against this system. All this is the result of your past sins; what can be done about it? Bear it silently! and with such kinds of sleeping pills, they wereable to buy peace for quite some time. But they were guilty of a great sin on this account since this amounted to the negation of core human values like self-esteem and self-reliance; grossly cruel conduct by all means. Yet the present is the moment of its atonement.

From a broader social perspective, untouchability had a malignantside-effect; people, in general, got used to hating the jobs which were otherwise vital for life. We treated the weavers who provided us with clothes as untouchable. In U.P. water carriers are also considered untouchables. All this caused immense damage to our progress by undermining the dignity of labour, especially manual labour. We have to accept it therefore, once and for all, that in order to move forward we have to give up both considering and calling them untouchables.

Everything else shall fall in place by itself.

In this regard strategy adopted by Naujwan Bharat Sabha and the Youth Conference is most suitable, that is, seeking forgiveness from those brethren, whom we have been calling untouchables by treating them as our fellow beings, without making them go through conversion ceremonies of Sikhism, Islam or Hinduism, by accepting food / water from their hands. And quarrelling among ourselves in the race to win them over, without restoring to them their human dignity is futile.

But the moment we went to villages with our message of human equality and brotherhood mentioned above, Government agents started rousing the Jat community saying that this would encourage these menials to decline serving you. This was sufficient to incite the jats, to oppose our efforts in the right direction.

But the upper castes should also realise that their own status in life cannot change for the better as long as they continueconsidering these people as inferiors, calling them menials, and keeping them under their heels. It is arguedthat they are unclean. The harsh truth is that they are poor; remove their poverty and they shall be clean. Don't we find that the poor even among the upper castes are no less unclean? Besides doing unclean jobs is not bad;

for example, mothers perform all the unclean duties for their children. Do they become unclean?

However, ultimately the problem can not be adequately solved unless and until untouchable communities themselves unite and organize. We regard their recent uniting to form their distinct identity, and also demanding representation equal to Muslims in legislatures, being equal to them in number, as a move in the right direction. Either reject communal representation altogether, else give these people their due shareas well! In principle, Councils, Assemblies are obligated to ensure full and free access to schools, colleges, wells and roads to all these communities; that too not only on paper but by actually accompanying them to wells, and schools and getting them admitted there. But can these legislatures, where a lot of hue and cry is made even over a bill to ban child marriageon grounds that it shall be a threat to their religion, dare to bring the untouchables to their own level by themselves? No, never, that is why we plead that they must persevere in pressing for their own distinct representation in legislatures in proportion to their numerical strength. We mince no words in proclaiming: Arise! So-called untouchables, the real sustainers of life, awake and reflect over your past, you were the backbone of Guru Gobind Singh's army. Shivaji was able to achieve all that with your participation which made him ever shining in history. Your sacrifices are worthy of being embedded in golden letters. The way in which you sustain us and add to our comforts ought to make us feel grateful to you. It is we who fail to appreciate. The land Alienation Act (banning transfer of land to non-agriculturist communities, defined as per caste) does not permit you to buy land even if you manage the required amount to bear its cost. The way you are being oppressed had prompted Miss Mayo of the U.S.A. to label you "less than man." As a matter of fact, without your own efforts, you shall not be able to move ahead.

"Those who would be free must themselves strike the first blow." It must be kept in mind that everyone belonging to the privileged class, strives to enjoy his own rights, but would try his utmost to continue oppressing those below him, and keeping the underprivileged beneath his heel. This might is held to be right. Then waste no time and unite to stand on your own feet and challenge the existing order of society. Let it then be seen as to who dares to deny to you your due. Do not be at the mercy of others and have no delusions about them. Be on guard so as not to fall into the trap of bureaucracy, because far from being your ally it seeks to make you dance to its tunes. The capitalist bureaucratic combination is, truly speaking, responsible for your oppression and poverty. Hence always shun it. Be on guard about its tricks. This is then the way out. You are the real working class. Workers unite – you have nothing to lose but your chains. Arise and rebel against the existing order. Gradualism and reformism shall be of no avail to you. Start a revolution from a social agitation and gird up your loins for political and economic revolution. You and you alone are the pillars of the nation, its real strength. O sleeping lions! Wake up and raise the banner of revolt.

3.

Blood Sprinkled on the Day of Holi Babbar Akalis on the Crucifix

In 1925-26 Bhagat Singh was at Kanpur, working under Ganesh Shankar Vidyarthi in the Hindi weekly *Partap*. While at Kanpur he wrote this articleabout the martyrs of Babbar Akali movement and signed it as Ek Punjabi Yuvak (a Punjabi youth).It was published in *Pratap* on March 15, 1926.

ON THE DAY OF HOLI, FEBRUARY 27, 1926, WHEN WE were getting high on our enjoyment, a terrible thing was happening in a corner of this great province. When you will hear it, you will shudder! You will tremble! On that day, six brave Babbar Akalis were hanged in the Lahore Central Jail. Shri Kishan Singhji Gadagajja, Shri Santa Singhji, Shri Dilip Sinhghji, Shri Nand Singhji, Shri Karam Singhji and Shri Dharam Singhji, had been showing a great indifference to the trial for the last two years, which speaks of their fond waiting for this day. After months, the judge gave his verdict. Five to be hanged, many for life imprisonment or exile, and sentences of very long imprisonments. The accused heroes thundered. Even the skies echoed with their triumphant slogans. Then an appeal was prefered. Instead of five, now six were sent to the noose. The same day the news came that a mercy petition was sent. The Punjab Secretary declared that the hanging would be put off. We were waiting but, all of a sudden, on the very day of Holi, we saw a small contingent of mourners carrying the dead bodies of the heroes towards the cremation site. Then last rites were completed quietly.

The city was still celebrating. Colour was still being thrown on the passers-by. What a terrible indifference. If they were misguided, if they were frenzied, let them be so. They were fearless patriots, in any case. Whatever they did, they did it for this wretched country. They could not bear injustice. They could not countenance the fallen nation. The oppression on the poor people became insufferable for them. They could not tolerate exploitation of the masses, they challenged and jumped into action. They were full of life. Oh! the terrible toll of their dedicated deeds! You are blessed! After death, friends and foes are all alike-this is the ideal of men. Even if they might have done something hateful, their lives at the altar of our nation, is something to the opposite side, could highly and uninhibitedly appreciate the courage, patriotism and commitment of the brave revolutionary of Bengal, Jatin Mukherjee, while mourning his death. But we the cowards and human wretches lack the courage of even sighing and putting off our celebrations even for a moment. What a disheartening deed! The poor! they were given the "adequate" punishment even by the standard of the brutal bureaucrats. An act of a terrible tragedy thus ended, but the curtain is not down as yet. The drama will have some more terrible scenes. The story is quite lengthy, we have to turn back a little to know about it.

The Non-Cooperation Movement was at its peak. The Punjab did not lag behind. The Sikhs also rose from their deep slumber and it was quite an awakening. The Akali Movement was started. Sacrifices were made in abundance. Master Mota Singh, ex-teacher of Khalsa Middle School, Mahalpur (district Hoshiarpur), delivered a speech. A warrant was issued against him, but the idea of availing of the hospitality of the crown did not find his favour. He was against offering arrest to fill the jails. His speeches still continued. In Kot-Phatuhi village, a big 'Deevan' was called. Police cordoned the area off from all sides; even then Master Mota Singh delivered his speech. The whole audience stood up and dispersed on the orders of the persident of the meeting. The Master escaped mysteriously. This hide-and-seek continued for long. The government was in a frenzy. At last, a friend turned traitor, and Master Saheb was arrested after a year and a half. This was the first scene of that horrible drama.

The "Guru ka bagh" movement was started. The hired hoodlums were there to attack the unarmed heroes and to beat them half-dead. Could anyone who looked at or listened to this, help being moved? It was a case of arrests and arrests everywhere. A warrant was also issued against Sardar Kishan Singhji Gadagajja, but he also belonged to the same category and did not offer arrest. The police strained all its nerves but he always escaped. He had an organisation of his own. He could not bear the violence against unarmed agitators. He felt the need of using arms along with this peaceful movement.

On the one hand, the dogs, the hunting dogs of the government, were searching for the clues, to get his scent; on the other, it was decided to "reform" the sycophants (Jholi Chukkas). Sardar Kishan Singhji used to say that we must keep ourselves armed for our own security, but we should not take any precipitate action for the time being. The majority was against this. At last, it was decided that three of them should give their names, take all the blame on themselves and start reforming these sycophants. Sardar Karam Singhji, Sardar Dhanna Singhji and Sardar Uday Singhji stepped forward. Just keep aside the question of its propriety for a moment and imagine the scene when they took the oath:

We will sacrifice our all in the service of the country. We swear to die fighting but not to go to the prison.

What a beautiful, sanctified scene it must have been, when these people who had given up all of their family affections, were taking such an oath! Where is the end of sacrifice? Where is the limit to courage and fearlessness? Where does the extremity of idealism reside?

Near a station on Shyam Churasi-Hoshiarpur railway branch line, a Subedar became the first victim. After that, all these three declared their names. The government tried its best to arrest them, but failed. Sardar Kishan Singh Gadagajja was once almost trapped by the police near Roorki Kalan. A young man who accompanied him, fell down after getting injured, and was captured. But even there, Kishan Singhji escaped with the help of his arms. He met a Sadhu on the way who told him about a herb in his possession which could materialise all his plans and work miracles. Sardarji believed him and visited this Sadhu unarmed. The Sadhu gave him some herbs to prepare and brought the police in the meanwhile. Sardar Saheb was arrested. That Sadhu was an inspector of the CID department. The Babbar Akalis stepped up their activities. Many pro-government men were killed. The doab land lying in between Beas and Sutlej, that is, the districts of Jullundur and Hoshiarpur, had been there on the political map of the country, even before this. The majority of martyrs of 1915 belonged to these districts. Now again, there was the upheaval. The police department used all its power at its command, which proved quite useless. There is a small river near Jullundur; "Chaunta Sahib" Gurudwara is located there in a village on the banks of the river. There Shri Karam Singhji,

Shri Dhanna Singhji, Shri Uday Singhji and Shri Anoop Singhji were sitting with a few others, preparing tea. All of a sudden, Shri Dhanna Singhji said: "Baba Karam Singhji! We should at once leave this place. I sense something very inauspicious happening." The 75-year old Sardar Karam Singh showed total indifference, but Shri Dhanna Singhji left the place, along with his 18-year old follower Dilip Singh. Quite suddenly Baba Karam Singh stared at Anoop Singh and said: "Anoop Singh, you are not a good person", but after this, he himself became unmindful of his own premonition. They were still talking when police made a declaration: Send out the rebels, otherwise the village will be burnt down. But the villagers did not yield.

Seeing all this, they themselves came out. Anoop Singh ran with all the bombs and surrendered. The remaining four people were standing, surrounded from all sides. The British police captain said: "Karam Singh! drop the weapons and you will be pardoned." The hero responded challengingly: "We will die a martyr's death while fighting, as a real revolutionary, for the sake of our motherland, but we shall not surrender our weapons." He inspiringly called his comrades. They also roared like lions. A fight ensued. Bullets flew in all directions. After their ammunition exhausted, these brave people jumped into the river and bravely died after hours of ceaseless fighting.

Sardar Karam Singh was 75 years old. He had been in Canada. His character was pure and behaviour ideal. The government concluded that the Babbar Akalis were finished, but actually they grew in strength. The 18-year old Dilip Singh was a very handsome and strong, well-built, though illiterate, young man. He had joined some dacoit gang. His association with Shri Dhanna Singhji turned him from a dacoit into a real revolutionary. Many notorious dacoits like Banta Singh and Variyam Singh, too, gave up dacoity and joined them.

There were not afraid of death. They were eager to wash their old sins. They were increasing in number day-by-day. One day when Dhanna Singh was sitting in a village named. Mauhana, the police was called. Dhanna Singh was down with drinks and caught without resistance. His revolver was snatched, he was handcuffed and brought out. Twelve policemen and two British officers had surrounded him. Exactly at that moment there was a thunderous noise of explosion. It was the bomb exploded by Dhanna Singhji. He died on the spot along with one British officer and ten policemen. All the rest were badly wounded.

In the same fashion, Banta Singh, Jwala Singh and some others were surrounded in a village named Munder. They all were gathered on the roof of a house. Shots were fired, a cross-fire ensued for some time, but then the police sprinkled kerosene oil by a pump and put the house on fire. Banta Singh was killed there, but Variyam Singh escaped even from there.

It will not be improper here to describe a few more similar incidents. Banta Singh was a very courageous man. Once he snatched a horse and a rifle from the guard of the armoury in the Jullundur Cantonment. Those days several police squads were desperately looking for him; one such squad confronted him somewhere in the forest. Sardar Saheb challenged them immediately: "If you have courage, come and confront me." On that side, there were slaves of money; on this side, the willing sacrifice of life. There was no comparison of motives. The police squad beat a retreat.

This was the condition of the special police squads deputed to arrest them. Anyway, arrests had become a routine. Police checkposts were erected in almost every village. Gradually, the Babbar Akalis were weakened. Till now it had seemed as if they were the virtual rulers. Wherever they happened to be visiting, they were warmly hosted, by some with fear and terror. The supporters of the regime were defeatist. They lacked the courage to move out of their residences between the sunset and the sunrise. They were the 'heroes' of the time. They were brave and their worship was believed to be a kind of hero-worship, but gradually they lost their strength. Hundreds among them were imprisoned, and cases were instituted against them.

Variyam Singh was the lone survivor. He was moving towards Layallpur, as the pressure of police had increased in Jullundur and Hoshiarpur. One day he was hopelessly surrounded there, but he came out fighting valiantly. He was very much exhausted. He was alone. It was a strange situation. One day he visited his maternal uncle in the village named Dhesian. Arms were kept outside. After taking his meals, he was moving towards his weaponry when the police arrived. He was surrounded. The British officer caught him from the backside. He wounded him badly with his kripan (sword), and he fell down. All the efforts to handcuff him failed. After two years of suppression, the Akali Jatha came to an end. Then the cases started, one of which has been discussed above. Quite recently too, they had wished to be hanged soon. Their wish has been fulfilled; they are now quiet.

4.

Religious Riots and their Solution

After the JallianwalaBagh tragedy in 1919, the British began propaganda to incite communal riots and Kohat in 1924 saw huge riots. After this, there was considerable debate on communal riots in the national political arena. The Congress leaders made an attempt to get Hindu and Muslim leaders to sign a pact to stop the riots. This piece was written by Bhagat Singh in this context and was published in the June 1927 issue of *Kirti*.

The conditions in India are indeed in a sorry state today. The followers of one religion are avowed enemies of the followers of another religion. Now, to belong to one religion alone is considered enough reason to be the enemy of another. If we find it unbelievable, let us see the fresh outbursts of violence in Lahore. How the Muslims slayed innocent Sikhs and Hindus, and how the Sikhs did even worse when the chance came. This slaughtering did not take place because a specific man committed a crime, but because that particular man is a Hindu or a Sikh or a Muslim. Only the fact that a person is a Sikh or a Hindu is enough for him to be killed by a Muslim, and similarly, being a Muslim, merely, is a worthwhile reason to take his life. If this is the condition, then may God help Hindustan!

Under these circumstances, Hindustan's future seems very bleak. These 'religions' have taken the country to its ruins. And one has no clue for how long these religious riots will afflict Hindustan. There riots have smeared Hindustan's name in front of the entire world. And we have seen how people get carried away by the tide of blind faith. It is rare to find a Hindu, Muslim or Sikh who can keep a cool head; all others take up sticks and staffs, swords and knives and kill each other. Those who cheat death either go to the gallows or are thrown into jail. After ample bloodshed, only when these 'religious' folk are subjected to the baton of the English government, do they come to their senses.

Insofar as we have seen, communal leaders and newspapers are behind these riots. Nowadays the Indian leaders show such disgraceful conduct that it is better not to say anything. The same leaders who have taken upon themselves the challenge of gaining independence for their country and who do not get weary of shouting slogans of 'Common Nationality' and 'Self Rule… Self-Rule…' are hiding and are surfing along this tide of religious blindness. The number of people screening themselves is much less. But if you dig deeper, leaders who are joining communal agitations can be found in hundreds. Only a handful of leaders are there who desire welfare of people from the bottom of their hearts. Communalism has come like such a great flood that they are not able to curtail it. It appears as if the leadership of Bharat has gone in dire straits.

The other persons who have played a distinct role in kindling communal riots are the ones working with newspapers.The profession of journalism, which was once accorded a very high status has turned very soiled now. These people print conspicuous, provocative headlines and incite the passions of people against one another that causes rioting. Not just in one or two places, but in many places, riots have occurred because the local papers have printed very outrageous essays. Few writers have been able to uphold their rationality and keep calm on such days.

The actual duty of the newspapers was to impart education, eradicate bigotry in people, end communal feelings, encourage mutual understanding, and create a common Indian nationalism. But they have twisted their responsibilities to spreading ignorance, preaching narrow-mindedness, creating biases, causing rioting and extinguishing Indian common nationalism. This is the reason that tears of blood flow from our eyes at Bharat's current state and the question that rises in our hearts is, 'What will become of Hindustan?'

Class-consciousness is critical to stopping people from fighting each other. The poor workers and peasants should be made to understand clearly that their actual enemies are the capitalists, so they must be cautious to not fall into their trap. All the poor people of the world – irrespective of their caste, race, religion or nation – have the same rights. It is in your interest that all discrimination on account of religion, colour, race, and nationality is removed and the power of the government be taken into your hands. These efforts will not harm you in any way, but will one day cut off your shackles and you will get economic freedom.

The people who are familiar with the history of Russia know that similar conditions prevailed there during the rule of the Tsar. There were several groups who kept dragging each other down. But from the day the Workers' Revolution took place, the very map of the place changed. Now riots do not ever take place there. Now, everybody there is considered a 'human being' and not a 'member of a religious group'. The economic condition of the people was very pitiful during the times of the Tsar which led to rioting. But now when the economic condition of the Russians improved, when they developed class-consciousness, there is no news of riots from there.

Though all one hears of the riots are agonizing accounts but we heard something positive about the Calcutta riots. The workers of the trade unions did not participate in the riots nor did they come to blows with each other; on the other hand, all the Hindus and Muslims behaved normally towards each other in the mills and even tried to stop the riots. This is because there was class-consciousness in them and they fully recognized what would benefit their class. This is the magnificent path of class-consciousness that can stop communal rioting.

We have heard this joyous news that the youth of India are now bolting away from those religions which teach hatred and communal violence. They have become so forward in their outlook that they do not see people as Hindus, Muslims or Sikhs, but first as human beings and then as Indians. With the rise of these thoughts in the youth of India, I see hope for the future of India. Indians should not get upset at the news of these riots, but they should pursue not building a communal environment which results in riots. The martyrs of 1914-15 had separated religion from politics. They understood that religion is a personal matter of an individual where no interference is needed from another. But they all agreed that religion should not enter politics as it does not allow people to work together for a common cause. This was the reason why during the revolution called by Gadar Party, people remained united. Here Sikhs, Hindus and Muslims were put on gallows for the cause of revolution. Today there are new politicians who have entered the fight for freedom, who want to separate religion from politics. This is a beautiful way to cure the malaise of communal violence. Even though we have different religious beliefs, if we separate religion from politics we all can stand together in the matter of politics and national cause. We hope that the true sympathizers of India will think over our solutions and will save India from following the path of self-destruction.

5.

Beware, Ye Bureaucracy

A handwritten leaflet,written on December 18, 1928 in Mozang House Den,explaining the reasons for Saunders' murder. It was pasted at several places on the walls of Lahore in the night between the 18th and 19th. A copy in Bhagat Singh's handwriting was produced as an exhibit in the Lahore Conspiracy Case.

HINDUSTAN SOCIALIST REPUBLICAN ARMY NOTICE

J.P. Sunders is dead; Lala Lajpat Rai is avenged

Really it is horrible to imagine that so lowly and violent hand of an ordinary Police Official, J.P. Saunders could ever dare to touch in such an insulting way the body of one so old, so revered and so loved by 300 millions of people of Hindustan and thus cause his death. The youth and manhood of India was challenged by blows hurled down on the head of the India's nationhood. And let the world know that India still lives; that the blood of youths has not been totally cooled down and that they can still risk their lives, if the honour of their nation is at stake. And it is proved through this act by those obscure who are ever persecuted, condemned and denounced even by their own people.

Beware, Ye Tyrants; Beware

Do not injure the feeling of a downtrodden and oppressed country. Think twice before perpetrating such diabolical deed, And remember that despite 'Arms Act' and strict guards against the smuggling of arms, the revolvers will ever continue to flow in–if not sufficient at present for an armed revolt, then at least sufficient to avenge the national insults. Despite all the denunciations and condemnation of their own kiths and kins, and ruthless repression and persecution of the alien government, party of young men will ever live to teach a lesson to the haughty rulers. They will be so bold as to cry even amidst the raging storm of opposition and repression, even on the scaffold:

"LONG LIVE THE REVOLUTION"!

Sorry for the death of a man. But in this man has died the representative of an institution which is so cruel, lowly and so base that it must be abolished. In this man has died an agent of the British authority in India - the most tyrannical of Govt. of Govts. In the world.

Sorry for the bloodshed of a human being; but the sacrifice of individuals at the altar of the Revolution that will bring freedom to all and make the exploitation of man by man impossible, is inevitable.

"Long Live Revolution"!

Balraj

Dated: 18th December, 1928

6.

Letter to Shaheed Sukhdev

(April 5, 1929)

This letter was written on April 5, 1929 in Sita Ram Bazar House, Delhi. The letter was taken to Lahore by Shri Shiv Verma and handed over to Sukhdev and was recovered from him at the time of his arrest on April 13 and was produced as one of the exhibits in Lahore Conspiracy Case. It reflects Bhagat Singh's views on the question of love and sacrifice in the life of a revolutionary.

DEAR BROTHER

By the time you receive this letter I will be gone, going to a far off destination. Let me assure that I am prepared for the voyage inspite of all the sweet memory and inspite of all the charms of my life here. Upto this day one thing pinched in my heart and it was this that my brother, my own brother, misunderstood and accused me of a very serious charge—the charge of weakness. Today I am quite satisfied, today more than ever do I feel that was nothing, but a misunderstanding, a wrong calculation. My overfrankness was interpreted as my talkativeness, and my confession as my weakness. And now I feel it was misunderstanding and only is understanding. I am not weak, not weaker than anyone amongest us, brother. With a clear heart I go, will you clear too? It will be very kind of you. But note that you are to take no hasty step, soberly and calmly you are to carry on the work. Don't try to take the chance at the very outset. You have some duty towards the public, and that you can fulfil by continuing this work. As a suggestion I would say that M.R. Shastri appeals to me more than ever. Try to bring him in the arena, provided he himself may be willing, clearly knowing the dark future. Let him mix with men and study their psychology. If he will work in the right spirit, he will be the better judge. Arrange as you may deem fit. Now, brother, let us be happy.

By the way, I am say that I cannot help arguing once again my case in the matter under discussion. Again do I emphasise that I am full of ambition and hope and of full charm of life. But I can renounce all at the time of need, and that is the real sacrifice. These things can never be hindrance in the way of man, provided he be a man. You will have the practical proof in the near future. While discussing anybody's character you asked me one thing, whether love ever proved helpful to any man. Yes, I answer that question today. To Mazzini it was. You must have read that after the utter failure and crushing defeat of his first rising he could no bear the misery and haunting ideas of his dead comrades. He would have gone mad or committed suicide but for one letter of a girl he loved. He would as strong as any one, nay stronger than all. As regards the moral status of love I may say that it in itself is nothing but passion, not an animal passion but a human one, and very sweet too. Love in itself can never be an animal passion. Love always elevates the character of man. It never lowers him, provided love be love. You can't call these girls - mad people, as we generally see in films - lovers. They always play in the hands of animals passions. The true love cannot be created. It comes of its own accord, nobody can say when. It is but natural. And I may tell you that a young man and a young girl can love each other, and with the aid of their love they can overcome the passions themselves and can maintain their purity. I may clear one thing here; when I said that love has human weakness, I did not say it for an ordinary human being at this stage, where the people generally are. But that is most idealistic stage when man would overcome all these sentiments, the love, the hatred, and so on. When man will take reason as the sole basis of his activity. But at present it is not bad, rather good and useful to man. And moreove while rebuking the love. I rebuked the love of one individual for one, and that too in idealistic stage. And even then, man must have the strongest feelings of love which he may not confine to one individual and may make it universal. Now I think I have cleared my position. One thing I may tell you to mark; we inspite of all radical ideas that we cherish, have not been able to do away with the overidealistic Arya Samajist conception of morality. We may talk glibly about all the radical things that can possible be conceived, but in practical life we begin to tremble at the very outset. This I will request you do away with. And may I, Without fear at all the misapprehension in my mind, request you do kindly lower the standard of your over-idealism a bit, not to be harsh to those who will live behind and will be the victims of a disease as myself ? Don't rebuke them and thus add to their woes and miseries. They need your sympathy. May I repeat that you, without bearing any sort of grudge against any particular individual, will sympathise with those who needed the most ? But you cannot realise these things unless and until you yourself fall a victim to this. But, why I am writing all this? I wanted to be frank. I have cleared my heart. Wish you all success and happy life.

Yours.
B. S.

7.

The Leaflet thrown in the Central Assembly Hall

On April 8, 1929, the Viceroy's proclamation, enacting the two Bills, was to be made, despite the fact that the majority of members were opposed to it, and had rather rejected it earlier. Bhagat Singh and his comrade Batukeshwar Dutta bombed the session and showered copies of this leaflet. *"Inquilab Zindabad!"* became one of the most enduring slogans of the Indian Independence Movement. Bhagat Singh and Batukeshwar Dutta repeated the slogan at their June 1929 trial on charges related to the bomb-throwing incident. The leaflet was signed off as "Balraj",which was the pen name of Chander Shekhar Azad, but was primarily written by Bhagat Singh.

THE HINDUSTAN SOCIALIST REPUBLICAN ARMY (NOTICE)

"It takes a loud voice to make the deaf hear, with these immortal words uttered on a similar occasion by Valiant, a French anarchist martyr, do we strongly justify this action of ours."

"Without repeating the humiliating history of the past ten years of the working of the reforms (Montague-Chelmsford Reforms) and without mentioning the insults hurled at the Indian nation through this House-the so-called Indian Parliament-we want to point out that, while the people expecting some more crumbs of reforms from the Simon Commission, and are ever quarrelling over the distribution of the expected bones, the Government is thrusting upon us new repressive measures like the Public Safety and the Trade Disputes Bill, while reserving the Press Sedition Bill for the next session. The indiscriminate arrests of labour leaders working in the open field clearly indicate whither the wind blows."

"In these extremely provocative circumstances, the Hindustan Socialist Republican Association, in all seriousness, realizing their full responsibility, had decided and ordered its army to do this particular action, so that a stop be put to this humiliating farce and to let the alien bureaucratic exploiters do what they wish, but they must be made to come before the public eve in their naked form."

"Let the representatives of the people return to their constituencies and prepare the masses for the coming revolution, and let the Government know that while protesting against the Public Safety and Trade Disputes Bills and the callous murder of Lala Lajpat Rai, on behalf of the helpless Indian masses, we want to emphasize the lesson often repeated by history, that it is easy to kill individuals but you cannot kill the ideas Great empires crumbled while the ideas survived. Bourbons and Czars fell. While the revaluation marched ahead triumphantly."

"We are sorry to admit that we who attach so great a sanctity to human life, who dream of a glorious future, when man will be enjoying perfect peace and full liberty, have been forced to shed human blood. But the sacrifice of individuals at the altar of the 'Great Revolution' that will bring freedom to all, rendering the exploitation of man by man impossible, is inevitable."

"Long Live the Revolution."

Balraj

Commander-in-Chief

BOMB OUTRAGE IN AS BLY

TWO YOUTHS WITH REVOLVERS UNDER POLICE ARREST

House Disperses in Panic

SIR G. SCHUSTER, SIR B. DALAL AND OTHER M. L. As INJURED

"Red" Warning to Government

"YOU CAN KILL MEN BUT NOT IDEAS"

Headlines in a newspaper after the arrest of Bhagat Singh and Batukeshwar Dutt in Central Assembly Hall

Bomb shells recovered by CID from Lahore.
These became part of exhibits in the Assembly Bomb Case.
(Source: All India Roundup)

8.

Statement in the Session Court during Assembly Bomb Case

(June 6, 1929)

This is the statement given by Bhagat Singh and B.K. Dutt in the Assembly Bomb Case. It was read in the Court on June 6, 1929 by Mr. Asaf Ali on behalf of Bhagat Singh and B.K. Dutt.

We stand charged with certain serious offences, and at this stage it is but right that we must explain our conduct.

In this connection, the following questions arise.

1. Were the bombs thrown into Chamber, and, if so, why?

2. Is the charge, as framed by the Lower Court, correct or otherwise?

To the first half of first question, our reply is in the affirmative, but since some of the so-called 'eye witnesses' have perjured themselves and since we are not denying our liability to that extent, let our statement about them be judged for what it is worth. By way of an illustration, we many point out that the evidence of Sergeant Terry regarding the seizure of the pistol from one of us is a deliberate falsehood, for neither of us had the pistol at the time we gave ourselves up. Other witnesses, too, who have deposed to having seen bombs being thrown by us have not scrupled to tell lies. This fact had its own moral for those who aim at judicial purity and fairplay.

At the same time, we acknowledge the fairness of the Public Prosecutor and the judicial attitude of the Court so far.

Viceroy's Views Endorsed

In our reply to the next half of the first question, we are constrained to go into some detail to offer a full and frank explanation of our motive and the circumstances leading up to what has now become a historic event.

When we were told by some of the police officers, who visited us in jail that Lord Irwin in his address to the joint session of the two houses described the event as an attack directed against no individual but against an institution itself, we readily recognized that the true significance of the incident had been correctly appreciated.

We are next to none in our love for humanity. Far from having any malice against any individual, we hold human life sacred beyond words.

We are neither perpetrators of dastardly outrages, and, therefore, a disgrace to the country, as the pseudo-socialist Dewan. Chaman Lal is reported to have described us, nor are we 'Lunatics' as The Tribune of Lahore and some others would have it believed.

Practical Protest

We humbly claim to be no more than serious students of the history and conditions of our country and her aspirations. We despise hypocrisy, Our practical protest was against the institution, which since its birth, has eminently helped to display not only its worthlessness but its far-reaching power for mischief. They more we have been convinced that it exists only to demonstrate to world Indian's humiliation and helplessness, and it symbolizes the overriding domination of an irresponsible and autocratic rule. Time and again the national demand has been pressed by the people's representatives only to find the waste paper basket as its final destination.

Attack on Institution

Solemn resolutions passed by the House have been contemptuously trampled under foot on the floor of the so called Indian Parliament. Resolution regarding the repeal of the repressive and arbitrary measures have been treated with sublime contempt, and the government measures and proposals, rejected as unacceptable buy the elected members of the legislatures, have been restored by mere stroke of the pen. In short, we have utterly failed to find any justification for the existence of an institution which, despite all its pomp and splendour, organized with the hard earned money of the sweating millions of India, is only a hollow show and a mischievous make-believe. Alike, have we failed to comprehend the mentality of the public leaders who help the Government to squander public time and money on such a manifestly stage-managed exhibition of Indian's helpless subjection.

No Hope For Labour

We have been ruminating upon all these matters, as also upon the wholesale arrests of the leaders of the labour movement. When the introduction of the Trade Disputes Bill brought us into the Assembly to watch its progress, the course of the debate only served to confirm our conviction that the labouring millions of India had nothing to expect from an institution that stood as a menacing monument to the strangling of the exploiters and the serfdom of the helpless labourers.

Finally, the insult of what we consider, an inhuman and barbarous measure was hurled on the devoted head of the representatives of the entire country, and the starving and struggling millions were deprived of their primary right and the sole means of improving their economic welfare. None who has felt like us for the dumb driven drudges of labourers could possibly witness this spectacle with equanimity. None whose heart bleeds for them, who have given their life-blood in silence to the building up of the economic structure could repress the cry which this ruthless blow had wrung out of our hearts.

Bomb Needed

Consequently, bearing in mind the words of the late Mr. S.R. Das, once Law Member of the Governor - General's Executive Council, which appeared in the famous letter he had addressed to his son, to the effect that the 'Bomb was necessary to awaken England from her dreams', we dropped the bomb on the floor of the Assembly Chamber to register our protest on behalf of those who had no other means left to give expression to their heart-rending agony. Our sole purpose was "to make the deaf hear" and to give the heedless a timely warning. Others have as keenly felt as we have done, and from under the seeming stillness of the sea of Indian humanity, a veritable storm is about to break out. We have only hoisted the "danger-signal" to warn those who are speeding along without heeding the grave dangers ahead. We have only marked the end of an era of Utopian non-violence, of whose futility the rising generation has been convinced beyond the shadow of doubt.

Ideal Explained

We have used the expression Utopian non-violence, in the foregoing paragraph which requires some explanation. Force when aggressively applied is "violence" and is, therefore, morally unjustifiable, but when it is used in the furtherance of a legitimate cause, it has its moral justification. The elimination of force at all costs in Utopian, and the mew movement which has arisen in the country, and of that dawn we have given a warning, is inspired by the ideal which guided Guru Gobind Singh and Shivaji, Kamal Pasha and Riza Khan, Washington and Garibaldi, Lafayette and Lenin.

As both the alien Government and the Indian public leaders appeared to have shut their eyes to the existence of this movement, we felt it as our duty to sound a warning where it could not go unheard.

We have so far dealt with the motive behind the incident in question, and now we must define the extent of our intention.

No Personal Grudge

We bore no personal grudge or malice against anyone of those who received slight injuries or against any other person in the Assembly. On the contrary, we repeat that we hold human life sacred beyond words, and would sooner lay down our own lives in the service of humanity than injure anyone else. Unlike the mercenary soldiers of the imperialist armies who are disciplined to kill without compunction, we respect, and, in so far as it lies in our power, we attempt to save human life. And still we admit having deliberately thrown the bombs into the Assembly Chamber. Facts however, speak for themselves and our intention would be judged from the result of the action without bringing in Utopian hypothetical circumstances and presumptions.

No Miracle

Despite the evidence of the Government Expert, the bombs that were thrown in the Assembly Chamber resulted in slight damage to an empty bench and some slight abrasions in less than half a dozen cases, while

Government scientists and experts have ascribed this result to a miracle, we see nothing but a precisely scientific process in all this incident. Firstly, the two bombs exploded in vacant spaces within the wooden barriers of the desks and benches, secondly, even those who were within 2 feet of the explosion, for instance, Mr. P. Rau, Mr. Shanker Rao and Sir George Schuster were either not hurt or only slightly scratched. Bombs of the capacity deposed to by the Government Expert (though his estimate, being imaginary is exaggerated), loaded with an effective charge of potassium chlorate and sensitive (explosive) picrate would have smashed the barriers and laid many low within some yards of the explosion.

Again, had they been loaded with some other high explosive, with a charge of destructive pellets or darts, they would have sufficed to wipe out a majority of the Members of the Legislative Assembly. Still again we could have flung them into the official box which was occupied by some notable persons. And finally we could have ambushed Sir John Simon whose luckless Commission was loathed by all responsible people and who was sitting in the President's gallery at the time. All these things, however, were beyond our intention and bombs did no more than they were designed to do, and the miracle consisted in no more than the deliberate aim which landed them in safe places.

We then deliberately offered ourselves to bear the penalty for what we had done and to let the imperialist exploiters know that by crushing individuals, they cannot kill ideas. By crushing two insignificant units, a nation cannot be crushed. We wanted to emphasize the historical lesson that Lettres de cachets and Bastilles could not crush the revolutionary movement in France. Gallows and the Siberian mines could not extinguish the Russian Revolution. Bloody Sunday, and Black and Tans failed to strangle the movement of Irish freedom.

Can ordinances and Safety Bills snuff out the flames of freedom in India? Conspiracy cases, trumped up or discovered and the incarceration of all young men, who cherish the vision of a great ideal, cannot check the march of revolution. But a timely warning, if not unheeded, can help to prevent loss of life and general sufferings.

We took it upon ourselves to provide this warning and our duty is done.

(Bhagat Singh was asked in the lower court what he meant by word "Revolution". In answer to that question, he said) "Revolution" does not necessarily involve sanguinary strife nor is there any place in it for individual vendetta. It is not the cult of the bomb and the pistol. By "Revolution" we mean that the present order of things, which is based on manifest injustice, must change. Producers or labourers in spite of being the most necessary element of society, are robbed by their exploiters of the fruits of their labour and deprived of their elementary rights. The peasant who grows corn for all, starves with his family, the weaver who supplies the world market with textile fabrics, has not enough to cover his own and his children's bodies, masons, smiths and carpenters who raise magnificent palaces, live like pariahs in the slums. The capitalists and exploiters, the parasites of society, squander millions on their whims. These terrible inequalities and forced disparity of chances are bound to lead to chaos. This state of affairs cannot last long, and it is obvious, that the present order of society in merry-making is on the brink of a volcano.

The whole edifice of this civilization, if not saved in time, shall crumble. A radical change, therefore, is necessary and it is the duty of those who realize it to reorganize society on the socialistic basis. Unless this thing is done and the exploitation of man by man and of nations by nations is brought to an end, sufferings and carnage with which humanity is threatened today cannot be prevented. All talk of ending war and ushering in an era of universal peace is undisguised hypocrisy.

By "Revolution", we mean the ultimate establishment of an order of society which may not be threatened by such breakdown, and in which the sovereignty of the proletariat should be recognized and a world federation should redeem humanity from the bondage of capitalism and misery of imperial wars.

This is our ideal, and with this ideology as our inspiration, we have given a fair and loud enough warning.

If, however, it goes unheeded and the present system of Government continues to be an impediment in the way of the natural forces that are swelling up, a grim struggle will ensure involving the overthrow of all obstacles, and the establishment of the dictatorship of the dictatorship of the proletariat to pave the way for the consummation of the ideal of revolution. Revolution is an inalienable right of mankind. Freedom is an imperishable birth right of all. Labour is the real sustainer of society. The sovereignty of the ultimate destiny of the workers.

For these ideals, and for this faith, we shall welcome any suffering to which we may be condemned. At the altar of this revolution we have brought our youth as an incense, for no sacrifice is too great for so magnificent a cause. We are content, we await the advent of Revolution. "Long Live Revolution."

9.

Letter to I.G. (Prisons), Punjab

It is a prelude to a prolonged struggle in jail. The first letter was written to the authorities by Bhagat Singh pointing out the inadequacies of jails.

Mianwali Jail
17 June, 1929
To
The Inspector-General(Jails),
Punjab Jails,
Lahore

DEAR SIR,

Despite the fact that I will be prosecuted along with other youngmen arrested in Saunders shooting case, I have been shifted to Mianwali Jail from Delhi. The hearing of the case is to start from 26 June, 1929. I am totally unable to understand the logic behind this kind of shifting. Whatever it be, justice demands that every undertrial should be given all those facilities which help him to prepare and contest the case. How can I appoint any lawyer while I am here? It is difficult to keep on the contact with my father and other relatives. This place is quite isolated, the route is troublesome and it is very far from Lahore.

I request you that you order my immediate transfer to Lahore Central Jail so that I get an opportunity to prepare my case. I hope that it will be given the earliest consideration.

Yours truly
Bhagat Singh

10.

On the Slogan of 'Long Live Revolution'

Shri Ramanand Chaterji, the editor of *Modern Review*, ridiculed the slogan of "Long Live Revolution" through an editorial note. Bhagat Singh wrote a reply and handed it over to the trying magistrate to be sent to *Modern Review*. This was published in *The Tribune* on December 24, 1929.

To

THE EDITOR MODERN REVIEW

You have in the December (1929) issue of your esteemed magazine, written a note under the caption "Long Live Revolution" and have pointed out the meaninglessness of this phrase. It would be impertinent on our part to try to refute or contradict the statement of such an old, experienced and renowned journalist as your noble self, for whom every enlightened Indian has profound admiration. Still we feel it our duty to explain what we desire to convey by the said phrase, as in a way it fell to our lot to give these "cries" a publicity in this country at this stage.

We are not the originators of this cry. The same cry had been used in Russian revolutionary movement. Upton Sinclair, the well known socialist writer, has, in his recent novels Boston and Oil, used this cry through some of the anarchist revolutionary characters. The phrase never means that the sanguinary strife should ever continue, or that nothing should ever be stationary even for a short while. By long usage this cry achieves a significance which may not be quite justifiable from the grammatical or the etymological point of view, but nevertheless we cannot abstract from that the association of ideas connected with that. All such shouts denote a general sense which is partly acquired and partly inherent in them. For instance, when we shout "Long Live Jatin Das", we cannot and do not mean thereby that Das should Physically be alive. What we mean by that shout is that the noble ideal of his life, the indomitable spirit which enabled that great martyr to bear such untold suffering and to make the extreme sacrifice for that we may show the same unfailing courage in pursuance of our ideal. It is that spirit that we allude to.

Similarly, one should not interpret the word "Revolution" in its literal sense. Various meanings and significances are attributed to this word, according to the interests of those who use or misuse it. For the established agencies of exploitation it conjures up a feeling of blood stained horror. To the revolutionaries it is a sacred phrase. We tried to clear in our statement before the Session Judge, Delhi, in our trial in the Assembly Bomb Case, what we mean by the word "Revolution"

We stated therein that Revolution did not necessarily involve sanguinary strife. It was not a cult of bomb and pistol. They may sometimes be mere means for its achievement. No doubt they play a prominent part in some movements, but they do not - for that very reason -become one and the same thing. A rebellion is not a revolution. It may ultimately lead to that end.

The sense in which the word Revolution is used in that phrase, is the spirit, the longing for a change for the better. The people generally get accustomed to the established order of things and begin to tremble at the very idea of a change. It is this lethargical spirit that needs be replaced by the revolutionary spirit. Otherwise degeneration gains the upper hand and the whole humanity is led stray by the reactionary forces. Such a state of affairs leads to stagnation and paralysis in human progress. The spirit of Revolution should always permeate the soul of humanity, so that the reactionary forces may not accumulate (strength) to check its eternal onward march. Old order should change, always and ever, yielding place to new, so that one "good" order may not corrupt the world. It is in this sense that we raise the shout "Long Live Revolution".

Yours sincerely

Bhagat Singh

B. K. Dutt

11.

Hunger strikers' Demands

Bhagat Singh and B.K. Dutt were sentenced to transportation for life in the Delhi Assembly Bomb Case. After conviction, they were transferred to Mianwali and Lahore jails, respectively. They started a hunger strike for better treatment of political prisoners in jails. After a few days, Bhagat Singh was also shifted from Mianwali to Lahore Central Prison. They jointly addressed this letter to the Home Member, Government of India, enumerating their demands. From here started a period of prolonged struggle for better treatment of political prisoners in jails.

Central Jail Lahore

24.6.29

WE, BHAGAT SINGH AND B.K. DUTT, WERE SENTENCED to life transportation in the Assembly Bomb Case, Delhi, on the 19th April, 1929. As long as we were undertrial prisoners in Delhi Jail, we were accorded a very good treatment from that jail to the Mianwali and Lahore Central Jails respectively, we wrote an application to the higher authorities asking for better diet and a few other facilities, and refused to take the jail diet.

Our demands were as follows:

1. We, as political prisoners, should be given better diet and the standard of our diet should at least be the same as that of European prisoners. (It is not the sameness of dietary that we demand, but the sameness of standard of diet.)
2. We shall not be forced to do any hard and undignified labours at all.

3. All books, other than those proscribed, alongwith writing materials, should be allowed to us without any restriction.

4. At least one standard daily paper should be supplied to every political prisoner.

5. Political prisoners should have a special ward of their own in every jail, provided with all necessities as those of the europeans. And all the political prisoners in one jail must be kept together in that ward.

6. Toilet necessities should be supplied.

7. Better clothing.

We have explained above the demands that we made. They are the most reasonable demands. The Jail authorities told us one day that the higher authorities have refused to comply with our demands.

Apart from that, they handle us very roughly while feeding us artificially, and Bhagat Singh was lying quite senseless on the 10th June, 1929, for about 15 mts., after the forcible feeding, which we request to be stopped without any further delay.

In addition, we may be permitted to refer to the recommendations made in the U.P. Jail Committee by Pt. Jagat Narain and K.B. Hafiz Hidayat Hussain. They have recommended the political prisoners to be treated as "Better Class Prisoners."

We request you to kindly consider our demands at your earliest convenience.

-By "Political Prisoners", we mean all those people who are convicted for offences against the State, for instane the people who were convicted in the Lahore Conspiracy Cases, 1915-17, the Kakori Conspiracy Cases and Sedition Cases in general.

Yours

Bhagat Singh

B.K. Dutt

Bhagat Singh at Lahore Railway Police Station during his first arrest on May 29, 1927

12.

Message to Punjab Students' Conference

The Second Punjab Students' Conference was held in Lahore on October 19, 1929, under the presidency of Subhash Chandra Bose. Bhagat Singh grabbed the opportunity and sent this message asking the students to plunge whole-heartedly into the coming movement of 1930-31 and carry the message of revolution to the remotest corners of the country. It was jointly signed by B.K. Dutt. The message was read in the open session. It received thunderous applause from the students with the slogans of "Bhagat Singh Zindabad"!

COMRADES,

Today, we cannot ask the youth to take to pistols and bombs. Today, students are confronted with a far more important assignment. In the coming Lahore Session, the Congress is to give call for a fierce fight for the independence of the country. The youth will have to bear a great burden in this difficult times in the history of the nation. It is true that students have faced death at the forward positions of the struggle for independence. Will they hesitate this time in proving their same staunchness and self-confidence? The youth will have to spread this revolutionary message to the far corner of the country. They have to awaken crores of slum-dwellers of the industrial areas and villagers living in worn-out cottages, so that we will be independent and the exploitation of man by man will become an impossibility. Punjab is considered politically backward even otherwise. This is also the responsibility of the youth. Taking inspiration from the martyr Yatindra Nath Das and with boundless reverence for the country, they must prove that they can fight with steadfast resolve in this struggle for independence.

13.

Telegram on Lenin's Death Anniversary

On January 21, 1930, the accused in the Lahore Conspiracy Case appeared in court wearing red scarves. As soon as the magistrate took his chair they raised slogans "Long Live Socialist Revolution", "Long Live Communist International", "Long Live People""Lenin's Name Will Never Die", and "Down with Imperialism". Bhagat Singh then read the text of this telegram in the court and asked the magistrate to send it to the Third International.

ON LENIN DAY WE SEND HEARTY GREETINGS TO ALL who are doing something for carrying forward the ideas of the great Lenin. We wish success to the great experiment Russia is carrying out. We join our voice to that of the international working class movement. The proletariat will win. Capitalism will be defeated. Death to Imperialism.

14.

Hunger-Strikers' Demands Reiterated

The Lahore Conspiracy Case prisoners had suspended their hunger strike on the assurance that the Government of India was considering the Jail Committee Report and that the jail reforms would be punished for participating in the hunger strike. After the hunger strike was suspended, the GOI, however, resorted to delaying tactics. Disciplinary action was also taken against hunger strikers in U.P. and Punjab jails (other than LCC prisoners). It was in this connection that Bhagat Singh wrote this letter to the GOI, which was sort of a notice-cum-ultimatum for resuming the hunger strike.

The Home Member,

The Govt. of India, Delhi.

Through

The Special Magistrate,

Lahore Conspiracy Case, Lahore.

SIR,

With reference to our telegram dated 20th Jan. 1930, reading as follows, we have not been given any reply.

Home Member, India Government. Delhi Undertrials, Lahore Conspiracy Case and other Political Prisoners suspended hunger-strike on the assurance that the India Govt. was considering Provincial Jail Committee's reports. All India Government Conference over. No action yet taken. As vindictive treatment to political prisoners still continues, we request we be informed within a week final Govt. decision. Lahore Conspiracy Case undertrials.

As briefly stated in the above telegram, we beg to bring to your kind notice that the Lahore Conspiracy Case undertrials and several other political prisoners confined in Punjab jails suspended hunger strike on the assurance given by the members of the Punjab Jail Enquiry Committee that the question of the treatment of political prisoners was going to be finally settled to our satisfaction within a very short period. Further, after the death of our great martyr Jatindra Nath Das, the matter was taken up in the Legislative Assembly and the same assurance was given publicly by Sir James Crerar. It was then pronounced that there has been a change of heart and the question of the treatment of political prisoners was receiving the utmost sympathy of the government. Such political prisoners who were still on hunger strike in jails of the different parts of the country then suspended their hunger strike on the request being made to this effect in an AICC resolution passed in view of the said assurance and the critical condition of some of the prisoners.

Since then all the local governments have submitted their reports. A meeting of Inspectors- General of Prisons of different provinces has been held at Lucknow and the deliberations of the All-India Govt. Conference have been concluded at Delhi. The All-India Conference was held in the month of Dec. last. Over not carried into effect any final recommendations. By such dilatory attitude of the government we no less than the general public have begun to fear that perhaps the question has been shelved. Our apprehensions have been strengthened by the vindictive treatment meted out to hunger strikers and other political prisoners during the last four months. It is very difficult for us to know the details of the hardships to which the political prisoners are being subjected. Still the little information that has trickled out of the four walls of the jails is sufficient to furnish us with glaring instances. We give below a few such instances which we cannot but feel, are not in conformity with the govt. assurance.

(1) Sj. B.K. Banerji, undergoing 5 years imprisonment in connection with Dakshineshwar Bomb Case in Lahore Central Jail, joined the hunger strike last year. Now as a punishment for the same, for each day of his period of hunger strike, two days of the remission so far earned by him have been forfeited. Under usual circumstances his release was due in Dec. last, but it will be delayed by full four months. In the same Jail similar punishment has been awarded to Baba Sohan Singh, an old man of about seventy, now undergoing his sentence of life transportation in connection with the (first)

Lahore Conspiracy Case. Besides, among others, Sardar Gopal Singh confined in Mianwali Jail, Master Mota Singh confined in Rawalpindi Jail have also been awarded vindictive punishments for joining the general hunger strike. In most of these cases the periods of imprisonment have been enhanced while some of them have been removed from the Special class.

(2) For the same offence, i.e. joining the general hunger strike, Messrs. Sachindra Nath Sanyal, Ram Kishan Khattri and Suresh Chandra Bhattacharya, confied in Agra Central Jail, Raj Kumar Sinha, Sachindra Nath Bukshi, Manmath Nath Gupta and several other Kakori case prisoners have been severely punished. It is reliably learnt that Mr. Sanyal was given bar-fetters and solitary cell-confinement and as a consequence there has been a break-down in his health. His weight has gone down by eighteen pounds. Mr. Bhattacharya is reported to be suffering from tuberculosis. The three Bareilly Jail prisoners also have been punished. It is learnt that all their privileges have been withdrawn. Even their usual rights of interviewing with relations and communication with them were forfeited. They have all been considerably reduced in their weights. Two press statements have been issued in this connection in Sep. 1929 and Jan. 1930 by Pandit Jawaharlal Nehru.

(3) After the passing of the AICC resolution regarding hunger strike, the copies of the same, which were sent to different political prisoners, were withheld by the jail authorities. Further, the govt. refused a Congress deputation to meet the prisoners in this respect.

(4) The Lahore Conspiracy Case undertrials were assaulted brutally on 23rd and 24th Oct., 1929, by orders of high police officials. Full details have appeared in the press. The copy of the statement of one of us recorded by the Special Magistrate, Pt. Shri Krishan, has been duly forwarded to you in a communication dated 16th Dec., 1929 Neither the Punjab Government nor the Govt. of India felt it necessary to reply or even acknowledge receipt of our communication praying for an enquiry. While, on the other hand, local government has felt the imperative necessity of prosecuting us in connection with the very same incident for offering "violent" resistance".

(5) In the last week of Dec. 1929, Sj. Kiran Chandra Das and eight others confined in the Lahore Borstal Jail, when being taken to and produced in the Magistrate's Court, were found handcuffed and chained together in flagrant breach of the unanimous recommendations of the Punjab Jail Enquiry Committee and also of Inspector-General of Prisons, Punjab. It

is further noteworthy that these prisoners were undertrials, changed for a bailable offence. A long statement issued by Dr. Mohd. Aslam, Lala Duni Chand of Lahore and Lala Duni Chand of Ambala in this connection was published in Tribune.

When we learnt these and other sufferings of the political prisoners we refrained from resuming our hunger strike, though we were much grieved as we thought that the matter was going to be finally settled at an early date, but in the light of the above instances, are we now to believe that the untold sufferings of the hunger strikers and the supreme sacrifice made by Jatin Das have all been in vain? Are we to understand that the govt. gave its assurance only to check the growing tide of public agitation and to avert a crisis? You will agree with us if we say that we have waited patiently for a sufficiently reasonable period of time. But we cannot wait indefinitely. The government, by its dilatory attitude and the continuation of vindictive treatment to political prisoners, has left us no other option but to resume the struggle. We realise that to go on hunger strike and to carry it on is no easy task. But let us at the same time point out that India can produce many more Jatins and Wagias, Ran Rakshas and Bhan Singhs. (The last two named laid down their lives in the Andamans in 1917 - the first breathed his last after 63 days of hunger strike while the other died the death of a great hero after silently undergoing inhuman tortures for full six months.)

Enough has been said by us and the members of the public (inquiry committee) in justification of the better treatment of political prisoners and it is unnecessary here to repeat the same. We would however like to say a few words as regards the inclusion of motive as the basis and the most important factor in the matter of classification. Great fuss has been created on the question of criteria of classification. We find that motive has altogether been excluded so far from the criteria suggested by different provincial governments This is really strange attitude. It is through motive alone that the real value of any action can be decided. Are we to understand that the Government is unable to distinguish between a robber who robs and kills his victim and a Kharag Bahadur who kills a villain and saves the honour of a young lady and redeems society of a most licentious parasite? Are both to be treated as two men belonging to the same category? Is there no difference between two men who commit the same offence, one guided by selfish motive and the other by a selfless one? Similarly, is there no difference between a common murderer and a political worker, even if the latter resorts to violence? Does not his selflessness elevate his place from amongst those of ordinary criminals? In these circumstances we think that motive should be held as the most important factor in the criteria for classification.

Last year, in the beginning of our hunger strike, when public leaders including Dr. Gopi Chand and Lala Duni Chand of Ambala - the last named being one of the signatories to the Punjab Jail Enquiry Committee Report - approached us to discuss the same thing and when they told us that the government considered to treat the political prisoners convicted of offences of violent nature as Special class prisoners, then by way of compromise we agreed to the proposal to the extent of excluding those actually charged with murder. But, Later on, the discussion took a different turn and the communique containing the terms of reference for the Punjab Jail Enquiry Committee was so worded that the question of motive seemed to be altogether excluded, and the classification was based on two things:

(1) Nature of Offence; and

(2) Social Status of "Offender".

These criteria, instead of solving the problem, made it all the more complicated.

We could understand two classes amongst the political prisoners, those charged for non-violent offences and those charged for violent offences. But then creeps in the question of social status in the report of the Punjab Jail Enquiry Committee. As Chaudhary Afzal Haq has pointed out, and rightly too, in his note of dissent to this report, what will be the fate of those political workers who have been reduced to pauper's conditions due to their honorary services in the cause of freedom? Are they to be left at the mercy of a magistrate who will away try to prove the bonafide of his loyalty by classifying everyone as an ordinary convict? Or, is it expected that a non-cooperator will stretch his hand before the people against whom he is fighting as an opponent, begging for better treatment in jail? Is this the way of removing the causes of dissatisfaction, or rather intensifying them? It might be argued that people living in property outside the jails, should not expect luxuries inside the prison when they are detained for the purpose of punishment. But, are the reforms that are demanded, of a nature of luxury? Are they not the bare necessities of life, according to the most moderate standard of living? Inspite of all the facilities that can possibly be demanded, jail will ever remain a jail. The prison in itself does not contain and can never contain any magnetic power to attract the people from outside. Nobody will commit offences simply to come to jail. Moreover, may we venture to say that it is a very poor argument on the part of any government to say that its citizens have been driven to such extreme destitution that their standard of living has fallen even lower than that of jails? Does not such an argument cut at the very root of that government's right of existence? Anyhow, we are not concerned with that at present. What we want to say is that the best way to remove the prevailing dissatisfaction would be to classify the political prisoners as such into a separate class which may further be subdivided, if need be, into two classes - one for those convicted of nonviolent offences and the other for persons whose offences include violence. In that case motive will become one of the deciding factors. To say that motive cannot be ascertained in political cases is hypocritical assertion. What is it that today informs the jail authorities to deprive the 'politicals' even of the ordinary privileges? What it is that deprives them of the special grades or 'nambardaries', etc.? What does make the authorities to keep them aloof and separated from all other convicts? The same thing can help in the classification also.

As for the special demands, we have already stated them in full in our memorandum to the Punjab Jail Enquiry Committee. We would however particularly emphasise that no political prisoner, whatever his offence may be, should be given any hard and undignified labour for which he may not feel aptitude. All of them, confined in one jail, should be kept together in the same ward. At least one standard daily newspaper in vernacular or English should be given to them. Full and proper facilities for study should be granted. Lastly, they should be allowed to supplement their expenses for diet and clothing from their private sources.

We still hope that the government will carry into effect without further delay its promise made to us and to the public, so that there may not be another occasion for resuming the hunger strike. Unless and until we find a definite move on the part of the government to redeem its promise in the course of the next seven days, we shall be forced to resume the hunger strike.

Yours, etc.

Bhagat Singh, Dutt

& others

dated: 28th Jan., 1930 Undertrials, Lahore Conspiracy Case

15.

Reasons for Refusing to Attend the Court

The second hunger strike of the Lahore Conspiracy Case prisoners was also suspended after twenty-one days on the assurance given by the government. But there still remained issues and complaints that the magistrate did not listen to. The accused thereupon refused to attend court. *The Civil and Military Gazette* commented that the accused had boycotted the British court. This was wrong. Bhagat Singh contradicted it and explained the reasons for refusing to attend the court.

MISTER MAGISTRATE

After going through your order dated 4 February, 1930, which was published in The Civil and Military Gazette, it appears necessary that we explain to you the reason of our boycott of the court.

It is wrong to say that we have boycotted the courts of the British government. Today, we are going to the court of Mr. Louis who is hearing the case initiated against us under Section 22 of the Jail Act. We had presented our problems and difficulties in our bail application before you, but it still remains unconsidered.

Our comrades under trial belong to different and distant corners of the country. Therefore, they should be given the facility of meeting their wellwishers and sympathisers. Shri B.K. Dutt gave an application to meet Miss Lajjawati, and Shri Kamal Nath Tewari also wanted to meet someone, but were neither their relatives nor their lawyers. Even after securing their authorisation, they were not allowed to meet. It is quite clear from this that the undertrials are not given the facilities for their defence. Not merely this, Comrade Kranti Kumar, who was doing very useful work for our defence committee and was also providing us with things of daily use, has been imprisoned on a fabricated charge. It has come to our knowledge that when the fabricated charge of bringing bullets in the sauce, could not be proved against him, under Section 124 A in Gurudaspur which is distant from Lahore.

I myself cannot keep a wholetime lawyer: therefore I wanted that my trusted friends should observe the court proceedings by being present there, but they were denied permission without any explicit reason, and only Lala Amardas, Advocate, has been given a seat.

We can never like this drama acted in the name of justice, because we do not get any facility or benefit for defending ourselves. One more serious complaint is against non-available of newspapers. Undertrial prisoners cannot be treated like convicted prisoners. We should be given at least one newspaper regularly. We want one newspaper also for those who do not know English. Therefore, as a protest, we are returning even the English. Therefore, as a protest, we are returning even the English daily Tribune. We decided to boycott the court on 29 January, 1930, because of these complaints. We will rejoin the proceedings when these inconveniences are removed.

Yours

etc. etc.

16.

Statement Before the Lahore High Court Bench

Through this brilliant statement, Bhagat Singh demolished the basis of the Sessions Court judgement and emphasised the importance of motive. The motive of action, he argued, should be the main consideration while judging the offence of an accused.

MY LORDS,

We are neither lawyers nor masters of English language, nor holders of degrees. Therefore, please do not expect any oratorial speech from us. We therefore pray that instead of going into the language mistakes of our statement Your Lordships will try to understand the real sense of it.

Leaving other points to our lawyers, I will confine myself to one point only. The point is very important in this case. The point is as to what were our intentions and to what extent we are guilty. This is a very complicated question and no one will be able to express before you that height to mental elevation which inspired us to think and act in a particular manner. We want that this should be kept in mind while assessing our intentions our offence. According to the famous jurist Solomon, one should not be punished for his criminal offence if his aim is not against law.

We had submitted a written statement in the Sessions Court. That statement explains our aim and, as such, explains our intentions also. But the learned judge dismissed it with one stroke of pen, saying that "generally the operation of law is not affected by how or why one committed the offence. In this country the aim of the offence is very rarely mentioned in legal commentaries."

My Lords, our contention is that under the circumstances the learned judge ought to have judged us either by the result of our action or on the basis of the psychological part of our statement. But he did not take any of these factors into consideration.

The point to be considered is that the two bombs we threw in the Assembly did not harm anybody physically or economically. As such the punishment awarded to us is not only very harsh but revengeful also. Moreover, the motive knowing his psychology. And no one can do justice to anybody without taking his motive into consideration. If we ignore the motive, the biggest general of the words will appear like ordinary murderers; revenue officers will look like thieves and cheats. Even judges will be accused of murder. This way the entire social system and the civilisation will be reduced to murders, thefts and cheating. If we ignore the motive, the government will have no right to expect sacrifice from its people and its officials. Ignore the motive and every religious preacher will be dubbed as a preacher of falsehoods, and every prophet will be charged of misguiding crores of simple and ignorant people.

If we set aside the motive, then Jesus Christ will appear to be a man responsible for creating disturbances, breaking peace and preaching revolt, and will be considered to be a "dangerous personality" in the language of the law. But we worship him. He commands great respect in our hearts and his image creates vibrations of spiritualism amongst us. Why? Because the inspiration behind his actions was that of a high ideal. The rulers of that age could not recognise that high idealism. They only saw his outward actions. Nineteen centuries have passed since then. Have we not progressed during this period? Shall we repeat that mistake again? It that be so, then we shall have to admit that all the sacrifices of the mankind and all the efforts of the great martyrs were useless and it would appear as if we are still at the same place where we stood twenty centuries back.

From the legal point of view also, the question of motive is of special importance. Take the example of General Dyer. He resorted to firing and killed hundreds of innocent and unarmed people. But the military court did not order him to be shot. It gave him lakhs of rupees as award. Take another example. Shri Kharag Bahadur Singh, a young Gurkha, Killed a Marwari in Calcutta. If the motive be set aside, then Kharag Bahadur Singh ought to have been hanged. But he was awarded a mild sentence of a few years only. He was even released much before the expiry of his sentence. Was there any loophole in the law that he escaped capital punishment? Or, was the charge of murder not proved against him? Like us, he also accepted the full responsibility of his action, but he escaped death. He is free today. I ask Your Lordship, why was he not awarded capital punishment? His action was well calculated and well planned. From the motive end, his action was more serious and fatal than ours. He was awarded a mild punishment because his intentions were good. He was awarded a mild punishment because his intention were good. He saved the society from a dirty leach who had sucked the life-blood of so many pretty young girls. Kharag Singh was given a mild punishment just to uphold the formalities of the law.

This principle (that the law does not take motive into consideration - ed.) is quite absurd. This is against the basic principles of the law which declares that "the law is for man and not man for the law". As such, why the same norms are not being applied to us also? It is quite clear that while convicting Kharag Singh his motive was kept in mind, otherwise a murderer can never escape the hangman's noose. Are we being deprived of the ordinary advantage of the law because our offence is against the government, or because our action has a political importance?

My Lords, under these circumstances, please permit us to assert that a government which seeks shelter behind such mean methods has no right to exist. If it is exists, it is for the time being only, and that too with the blood of thousands of people on its head. If the law does not see the motive there can be no justice, nor can there be stable peace.

Mixing of arsenic (poison) in the flour will not be considered to be a crime, provided its purpose is to kill rats. But if the purpose is to kill a man, it becomes a crime of murder. Therefore, such laws which do not stand the test of reason and which are against the principle of justice, should be abolished. Because of such unjust laws, many great intellectuals had to adopt the path of revolt.

The facts regarding our case are very simple. We threw two bombs in the legislative Assembly on April 8, 1929. As a result of the explosion, a few persons received minor scratches. There was pandemonium in the chamber, hundreds of visitors and members of the Assembly ran out. Only my friend B.K. Dutt and myself remained seated in the visitors gallery and offered ourselves for arrest. We were tried for attempt to murder, and convicted for life. As mentioned above, as a result of the bomb explosion, only four or five persons were slightly injured and one bench got damaged. We offered ourselves for arrest without any resistance. The Sessions Judge admitted that we could have very easily escaped, had we had any intention like that. We accepted our offence and gave a statement explaining our position. We are not afraid of punishment. But we do not want that we should be wrongly understood. The judge removed a few paragraphs from our statement. This we consider to be harmful for our real position.

A proper study of the full text of our statement will make it clear that, according to us, our country is passing through a delicate phase. We saw the coming catastrophe and thought it proper to give a timely warning with a loud voice, and we gave the warning in the manner we throught proper. We may be wrong. Our line of thinking and that of the learned judge may be different, but that does not mean that we be deprived of the permission to express our ideas, and wrong things be propagated in our name.

In our statement we explained in detail what we mean by "Long Live Revolution" and "Down With Imperialism". That formed the crux of our ideas. That portion was removed from our statement. Generally a wrong meaning is attributed to the word revolution. That is not our understanding. Bombs and pistols do not make revolution. That is not our understanding. Bombs and pistols do not make revolution. The sword of revolution is sharpened on the whetting-stone of ideas. This is what we wanted to emphasise. By revolution we mean the end of the miseries of capitalist wars. It was not proper to pronounce judgement without understanding our aims and objects and the process of achieving them. To associate wrong ideas with our names is out and out injustice.

It was very necessary to give the timely warning that the unrest of the people is increasing and that the malady may take a serious turn, if not treated in time and properly. If our warning is not heeded, no human power will be able to stop it. We took this step to give proper direction to the storm. We are serious students of history. We believe that, had the ruling powers acted correctly at the proper time, there would have been no bloody revolutions in France and Russia. Several big power of the world tried to check the storm of ideas and were sunk in the atmosphere of bloodshed. The ruling people cannot change the flow of the current. We wanted to give the first warning. Had we aimed at killing some important personalities, we would have failed in the attainment of our aim.

My Lords, this was the aim and the spirit behind our action, and the result of the action corroborates our statement. There is one more point which needs elucidation, and that is regarding the strength of the bombs. Had we had no idea of the strength of the bombs, there would have been no question of our throwing them in the presence of our respected national leader like Pandit Motilal Nehru, Shri Kelkar, Shri Jayaker and Shri Jinnah. How could we have risked the lives of our leaders? After all we are not mad and, had we been so, we would have certainly been sent to the lunatic asylum, instead of being put in jail. We had full knowledge about the strength of the bombs and that is why we acted with so much confidence. It was very easy to have thrown the bombs on the occupied benches, but it was difficult to have thrown them on unoccupied seats. Had we not of saner mind or had we been mentally unbalanced, the bombs would have fallen on occupied benches and not in empty places. Therefore I would say that we should be rewarded for the courage we showed in carefully selecting the empty places. Under these conditions, My Lords, we think we have not been understood, My Lords, we think we have not been understood properly. We have not come before you to get our sentences reduced. We have come here to clarify our position. We want that we should not be given any unjust treatment, nor should any unjust opinion be pronounced about us. The question of punishment is of secondary importance before us.

17.

Regarding the Lahore Conspiracy Case Ordinance

The strategy of the Lahore Conspiracy Case prisoners was to prolong the case and use the court as a platform for propagating the objectives of the revolutionary party. The government understood their intention and expedited the proceedings. The government withdrew the case from the lower court and promulgated an ordinance known as the LCC Ordinance No. 3 of 1930. Equipped with the Ordinance, it appointed a Special Tribunal of three High Court judges, handed over the case to it and empowered it to dispense with the witnesses and proceed with the case even in the absence of the accused. The Governor-General, while justifying the step, said that the accused were resorting to hunger strikes again and again and were making it impossible for the court to proceed. It was in this context that Bhagat Singh wrote this letter to the Governor-General to demolish his argument.

To

His Excellency 2nd May, 1930

The Governor-General of India,

Simla,

Sir,

The full text of the special Ordinance to expedite our trial has been read over to us. To Tribunal has also been appointed by the Chief Justice of the Punjab High Court of Juridicature. We welcome the news. We could have kept silent, had you not referred to our attitude adopted so far in this case, and thus tried to throw the sole responsibility on our shoulders. In the present situation, we feel it necessary to make a statement to clear our position.

We have been marking from the very beginning that the Govt. authorities have always been trying to deliberately misrepresent us. After all, this is a fight, and the misrepresentation is and has always been the best instrument in the hands of the Govt. to meet their enemies. We have absolutely no grudge against this mean tactic. However, there are certain things the consideration of which is forcing us to make the following counter.

You have mentioned your statement issued alongwith the Lahore Conspiracy Ordinance, our hunger strike. As you have yourself admitted, two of us had begun the hunger strike weeks before the commencement of the inquiry into this case in the court of R.S Pt. Sri Krishan, Special Magistrate. Hence any man with the least common sense can understand that the hunger strike had nothing to do with the trial. The Govt. had to admit the existence of these grievances. When the Govt. made some gesture as to making certain arrangement for the settlement of this question, and Provincial Jail Enquiry Committees were appointed for the same purpose, we gave up the hunger strike. But at first we were informed that the question would be finally settled in November. Then it was postponed till December. But January also passed and there was not the least to indicate as to whether the Govt. was going to do anything in this connection at all, or not. We feared that the matter was shelved. Hence the second hunger strike on 4th Feb., 1930, after full one week's notice. It was only then that the Govt. tried to settle this question finally. A Communique was published and we again gave up the hunger strike and did not even wait to see the final decision, in this connection, carried into effect. It is only today that we are realising that the British Govt. has not yet given u the policy of telling lies even in such ordinary matters as this. This Communique is in specific terms, but we find something quite contrary in practice. Anyhow, this is not the proper place to discuss that question; we might have to deal with it later on, if the occasion arises. But what we want to emphasise here is that the hunger strike was never directed against the proceedings of the court. Such great sufferings cannot be invited and such great sacrifice cannot be made with that ordinary motive. Das did not lay down his life for such a trivial cause. Rajguru and others did not risk their lives simply to protract the trial.

You know thoroughly well, and everybody concerned knows it, that it is not hunger strike that has forced you to promulgate this Ordinance. There is something else the consideration of which confused the heads of your

Government it is neither the protraction of the case nor any other emergency which forces you to sign this lawless law. It is certainly something different.

But let us declare once and for all that our spirits cannot be cowed down by ordinances. You may crush certain individuals but you cannot crush this nation. As far as this Ordinance is concerned, we consider it to be our victory. We had been from the very beginning pointing out that this existing law was a mere make-believe. It could not administer justice. But even those privileges to which the accused were legitimately and legally entitled and which are given to ordinary accused were legitimately and legally entitled and which are given to ordinary accused, could not be given to the accused in political cases. We wanted to make the Govt. throw off its veil and to be candid enough to admit that fair chances for defence could not be given to the political accused. Here we have the frank admission of the Government. We congratulate you as well as your Govt. for this candour and welcome the Ordinance.

Insipte of the frank admission of your agents, the Special Magistrate and the Prosecution Counsels, as to the reasonableness of our attitude throughout, you had been confused at the very thought of the existence of our case. What else is needed to assure us of our success in this fight.

18.

Justice Hilton Must Also Go

On May 12, 1930, the presiding judge of the Special Tribunal lost his temper on the question of a song. He ordered that the accused be handcuffed. The accused were removed from the court by force and sent back to the jails. The accused boycotted the court from the next day onward and demanded that the presiding judge must apologise, on he should be removed.

On June 21 the presiding judge was removed, and on June 23 the accused went to the court to find Justice Hilton, who was a party to the order, presiding over the Tribunal. The accused objected to it and demanded that either Justice Hilton should dissociate himself from the order or he should apologise, failing which he should also be removed from the Tribunal. It was in this context that Bhagat Singh wrote this letter.

To

The Commissioner,

The Special Tribunal,

Lahore Conspiracy Case, Lahore.

SIR,

Whereas two judges of the Tribunal have withdrawn or have been made to withdraw themselves from the Tribunal and two new judges have been appointed in their place, we feel that a statement is very necessary on our part to explain our position clearly so that no misunderstanding may be possible.

It was on 12th May, 1930, that an order was passed by Mr. Justice Coldstream, the then President, to handcuff us in asking the court to inform us as to the cause of this sudden and extraordinary order was not thought worth consideration. The police handcuffed us forcibly and removed us back to jail. One of the three judges, Mr. Agha Harider, on the following day, dissociated himself with that order of the President. Since that day we have not been attending court.

Our condition on which we were prepared to attend court was laid before the Tribunal on the next day, namely that either the President should apologise or he should be replaced; by this we never meant that a judge who was a party to that order should take the place of the President.

For more than five weeks no heed was paid to the grievances of the accused.

According to the present formation of the Tribunal, both the President and the other judge who had dissociated himself from the order of the President, have been replaced by two new judges. Thus the judge who was a party to that order - as the President gave the order on behalf of the majority - has now been appointed the President of the Tribunal. In these circumstances we want to emphasise one thing that we had absolutely no grudge against the person of Mr. Justice Coldstream. We had protested against the order passed by the President on behalf of the majority and the subsequent maltreatment meted out to us. We have every respect for Mr. Justice Coldstream and Mr. Justice Hilton that should be expected from man to man. And as our protest was against a certain order we wanted the President to apologise, which meant apology by the President on behalf of the Tribunal who was responsible for that order. By the removal of the President the Position is not changed because Mr. Justice Hilton, who was a party to the order, is presiding in place position has added an insult to injury.

Yours, etc.

25th June, 1930 Bhagat Singh, B.K. Dutt

19.

Letter to Sukhdev on Suicide

While waiting for the judgement of their case, the primary question that troubled the minds of the accused was "what will happen to them?" Sukhdev, particularly was very dejected by the idea of life imprisonment. He would either be free or choose death. He wrote to Bhagat Singh that in case he is convicted for life, he will commit suicide. Bhagat Singh's reaction to Sukhdev's letter was very sharp. "Escaping from hardships is cowardice", he said. This letter remains crucial as it opens another window to peep into Singh's mind.

DEAR BROTHER,

I have gone through your letter attentively and many times. I realise that the changed situation has affected us differently. The things you hated outside have now become essential to you. In the same way, the things I used to support strongly are of no significance to me any more. For example, I believed in personal love, but now this feeling has ceased to occupy any particular position in my heart and mind. While outside, you were strongly opposed to it but now a drastic change and radicalisation is apparent in your ideas about it. You experience it as an extremely essential part of human existence and you have found a particular kind of happiness in the experience.

You may still recollect that one day I had discussed suicide with you. That time I told you that in some situations suicide may be justifiable, but you contested my point. I vividly remember the time and place of our conversation. We talked about this in the Shahanshahi Kutia one evening. You said in jest that such a cowardly act can never be justified. You said that acts of this kind were horrible and heinous, but I see that you have now made an about-turn on this subject. Now you find it not only proper in certain situations but also necessary, even essential. My opinion is what you had held earlier, that suicide is a heinous crime. It is an act of complete cowardice. Leave alone revolutionaries, no individual can ever justify such an act.

You say you fail to understand how suffering alone can serve the country. Such a question from a person like you is really perplexing, because how much thoughtfully we loved the motto of the Naujawan Bharat Sabha - "to suffer and sacrifice through service". I believe that you served as much as was possible. Now is the time when you should suffer for what you did. Another point is that this is exactly the moment when you have to lead the entire people.

Man acts only when he is sure of the justness of his action, as we threw the bomb in the Legislative Assembly. After the action, it is the time for bearing the consequences of that act. Do you think that had we tried to avoid the punishment by pleading for mercy, we would have been more justified? No, this would have had an adverse effect on the masses. We are now quite successful in our endeavour.

At the time of our imprisonment, the condition for the political prisoners of our party were very miserable. We tried to improve that. I tell you quite seriously that we believed we would die very shortly. Neither we were aware of the technique of forced feeding nor did we ever think of it. We were ready to die. Do you mean to say that we were intending to commit suicide? No. Striving and sacrificing one's life for a superior ideal can never be called suicide. We are envious of the death of our Comrade Yatindra Nath Das. Will you call it suicide? Ultimately, our sufferings bore fruit. A big movement started in the whole of the country. We were successful in our aim. Death in the struggles of this kind is an ideal death.

Apart from this, the comrades among us, who believe that they will be awarded death, should await that day patiently when the sentence will be announced and they will be hanged. This death will also be beautiful, but committing suicide - to cut short the life just to avoid some pain - is cowardice. I want to tell you that obstacles make a man perfect. Neither you nor I, rather none of us, have suffered any pain so far. That part of our life has started only now.

You will recollect that we have talked several times about realism in the Rusian literature, which is nowhere visible in our own. We highly appreciate the situations of pain in their stories, but we do not feel that spirit of suffering within ourselves. We also admire their passion and the extraordinary height of their characters, but we never bother to find out the reason. I will say that only the reference to their resolve to bear pain has produced the intensity, the suffering of pain, and this has given great depth and height to their characters and literature. We become pitiable and ridiculous when we imbibe an unreasoned mysticism in our life without any natural or substantial basis. People like us, who are proud to be revolutionary in every sense, should always be prepared to bear all the difficulties, anxieties, pain and suffering which we invite upon ourselves by the struggles initiated by us and for which we call ourselves revolutionary.

I want to tell you that in jail, and in jail alone, can a person get an occasion to study empirically the great social subjects of crime and sin. I have read some literature on this and only the jail is the proper place for the self-study on all these topics. The best parts of the self-study for one is to suffer oneself.

You know it that the suffering of political prisoners in the jails of Russia caused, in the main, the revolution in the prison-administration after the overthrow of Czardom. Is India not in need of such persons who are fully aware of this problem and have personal experience of these things? It will not suffice to say that someone else would do it, or that many other people are there to do it. Thus, men who find it quite dishonourable and hateful to leave the revolutionary responsibilities to others should start their struggle against the existing system with total devotion. They should violate these rules but they should also keep in mind the propriety, because unnecessary and improper attempts can never be considered just. Such agitations will shorten the process of revolution. All the arguments which you gave to keep yourself aloof from all such movement, are incomprehensible to me. Some of our friends are either fools or ignorant. They find your behaviour quite strange and incomprehensible. (They themselves say they cannot comprehend it because you are above and very far from their understanding.)

In fact, if you feel that jail life is really humiliating, why don't you try to improve it by agitating? Perhaps, you will say that this struggle would be futile, but this is precisely the argument which is usually used as a cover by weak people to avoid participation in every movement. This is the reply which we kept on hearing outside the jail from the people who were anxious to escape from getting entangled in revolutionary movements. Shall I now hear the same argument from you? What could our party of a handful of people do in comparison to the vastness of its aims and ideals? Shall we infer from this that we erred gravely in starting our work altogether? No, inferences of this kind will be improper. This only shows the inner weakness of the man who thinks like this.

You write further that it cannot be expected of a man that he will have the same thinking after going through 14 long years of suffering in the prison, which he had before, because the jail life will crush all his ideas. May I ask you whether the situation outside the jail was any bit more favourable to our ideas? Even then, could we have left it because of our failures? Do you mean to imply that had we not entered the field, no revolutionary work would have taken place at all? If this be your contention, then you are mistaken, though it is right that we also proved helpful to an extent in changing the environment. But, then, we are only a product of the need of our times.

I shall even say that Marx - the father of communism - did not actually originate this idea. The Industrial Revolution of Europe itself produced men of this kind. Marx was one among them. Of course, Marx was also instrumental to an extent in gearing up the wheels of his time in a particular way.

I (and you too) did not give birth to the ideas of socialism and communism in this country; this is the consequence of the effects of our time and situations upon ourselves. Of course, we did a bit to propagate these ideas, and therefore I say that since we have already taken a tough task upon ourselves, we should continue to advance it. The people will not be guided by our committing suicides to escape the difficulties; on the contrary, this will be quite a reactionary step.

We continued our work despite the testing environment of disappointments, pressures and violence ordained by the jail rules. While we worked, we were made target of many kinds of difficulties. Even men who were proud to proclaim themselves to be great revolutionaries, deserted us. Were these conditions not testing in the extreme? Then, what was the reason and the logic of continuing our agitation and efforts?

Does this simple argument not by itself give added strength to our ideas? And, don't we have instances of our revolutionary comrades who suffered for their convictions in jails and are still working on return from jails? Had

Bakunin argued like you, he would have committed suicide right in the beginning. Today, you find many revolutionaries occupying responsible posts in the Russian state who had passed the greater part of their lives in prison, completing their sentences. Man must try hard to stick to his beliefs. No one can say what future has in store.

Do you remember that when we were discussing that some concentrated and effective poison should also be kept in our bomb factories, you opposed it very vehemently. The very idea was repugnant to you. You had no faith in it. So, what has happened now? Here, even the difficult and complex conditions do not obtain. I feel revulsion even in discussing this question. You hated even that attitude of mind which permits suicide. You will kindly excuse me for saying that had you acted according to this belie right at the time of your imprisonment (that is, you had committed suicide by taking poison), you would have served the revolutionary cause, but at this moment, even the thought of such an act is harmful to our cause.

There is just one more point which I will like to draw your attention to. We do not believe in God, hell and heaven, punishment and rewards, that is in any Godly accounting of human life. Therefore, we must think of life and death on materialist lines. When I was brought here from Delhi for the purpose of identification, some intelligence officers talked to me on this topic, in the presence of my father. They said that since I did not try to save of my life by divulging secrets, it proved the presence of an acute agony in my life. They argued that a death of this kind will be something like suicide. But I had replied that a man with beliefs and ideal like mine, could never think of dying uselessly. We want to get the maximum value for our lives. We want to serve humanity as much as possible. Particularly a man like me, whose life is nowhere sad or worried, can never think of suicide even, leave alone attempting it. The same thing I want to tell you now.

I hope you will permit me to tell you what I think about myself. I am certain of capital punishment for me. I do not expect even a bit of moderation or amnesty. Even if there is amnesty, it will not be for all, and even that amnesty will be for other only, not for us; it will be extremely restricted and burdened with various conditions. For, us neither there can be any amnesty nor it will ever happen. Even then, I wish that release calls for us should be made collection and globally. Along with that, I also wish that when the movement reaches its climax, we should be hanged. It is my wish that if at any time any honourable and fair compromise is possible, issue like our case may never obstruct it. When the fate of the country is being decided, the fate of individuals should be forgotten. As revolutionaries, we do not believe that there can be any sudden change in the attitude of our rulers, particularly in the British race. Such a surprising change is impossible without through sustained striving, sufferings and sacrifices. And it shall be achieved. As far as my attitude is concerned, I can welcome facilities and amnesty for all only when its effect is permanent and some indelible impressions are made on the hearts of the people of the country through our hanging. Only this much and nothing more.

20.

Letter to Father

When the case was in its final stage,Bhagat Singh's father, Sardar Kishen Singh made a written request to the Tribunal, saying that there were many facts to prove that his son was innocent. He also requested that his son be allowed to prove his innocence. When Bhagat Singh came to know of it he was furious and wrote this convincing letter to his father, protesting against his move.

Oct. 4, 1930

MY DEAR FATHER,

I was astounded to learn that you had submitted a petition to the members of the Special Tribunal in connection with my defence. This intelligence proved to be too severe a blow to be borne with equanimity. It has upset the whole equilibrium of my mind. I have not been able to understand how you could think it proper to submit such a petition at this stage and in these circumstances. Inspite of all the sentiments and feelings of a father, I don't think you were at all entitled to make such a move on my behalf without even consulting me. You know that in the political field my views have always differed with those of yours. I have always been acting independently without having cared for your approval or disapproval.

I hope you can recall to yourself that since the very beginning you have been trying to convince me to fight my case very seriously and to defend myself properly. But you also know that I was always opposed to it. I never had any desire to defend myself and never did I seriously think about it. Whether it was a mere vague ideology or that I had certain arguments to justify my position, is a different question and that cannot be discussed here.

You know that we have been pursuing a definite policy in this trial. Every action of mine ought to have been consistent with that policy, my principle and my programme. At present the circumstances are altogether different, but had the situation been otherwise, even then I would have been the last man to offer defence. I had only one idea before me throughout the trial, i.e. to show complete indifference towards the trial inspite of serious nature of the charges against us. I have always been of opinion that all the political workers should be indifferent and should never bother about the legal fight in the law courts and should boldly bear the heaviest possible sentences inflicted upon them. They may defend themselves but always from purely political considerations and never from a personal point of view. Our policy in this trial has always been consistent with this principle; whether we were successful in that or not is not for me to judge. We have always been doing our duty quite disinterstedly.

In the statement accompanying the text of Lahore Conspiracy Case Ordinance the Viceroy had stated that the accused in this case were trying to bring both law and justice into contempt. The situation afforded us an opportunity to show to the public whether we were trying to bring law into contempt or whether others were doing so. People might disagree with us on this point. You might be one of them. But that never meant that such moves should be made on my behalf without my consent or even my knowledge. My life is not so precious, at least to me, as you may probably think it to be. It is not at all worth buying at the cost of my principles. There are other comrades of mine whose case is as serious as that of mine. We had adopted a common policy and we shall stand to the last, no matter how dearly we have to pay individually for it.

Father, I am quite perplexed. I fear I might overlook the ordinary principle of etiquette and my language may become a little but harsh while criticising or rather censoring this move on your part. Let me be candid. I feel as though I have been stabbed at the back. Had any other person done it, I would have considered it to be nothing short o treachery. But in your case, let me say that it has been a weakness - a weakness of the worst type.

This was the time where everybody's mettle was being tested. Let me say, father, you have failed. I know you are as sincere a patriot as one can be. I know you are as sincere a patriot as one can be. I know you have devoted your life to the cause of Indian independence, but why, at this moment, have you displayed such a weakness? I cannot understand.

In the end, I would like to inform you and my other friends and all the people interested in my case, that I have not approved of your move. I am still not at all in favour of offering any defence. Even if the court had accepted that petition submitted by some of my co-accused regarding defence, etc., I would have not defended myself. My applications submitted to the Tribunal regarding my interview during the hunger strike, were misinterpreted and it was published in the press that I was going to offer defence, though in reality I was never willing to offer any defence. I still hold the same opinion as before. My friends in the Borstal Jail will be taking it as a treachery and betrayal on my part. I shall not even get an opportunity to clear my position before them.

I want that public should know all the details about this complication, and, therefore, I request you to publish this letter.

Your loving son

Bhagat Singh

Kishen Singh, Bhagat Singh's father.

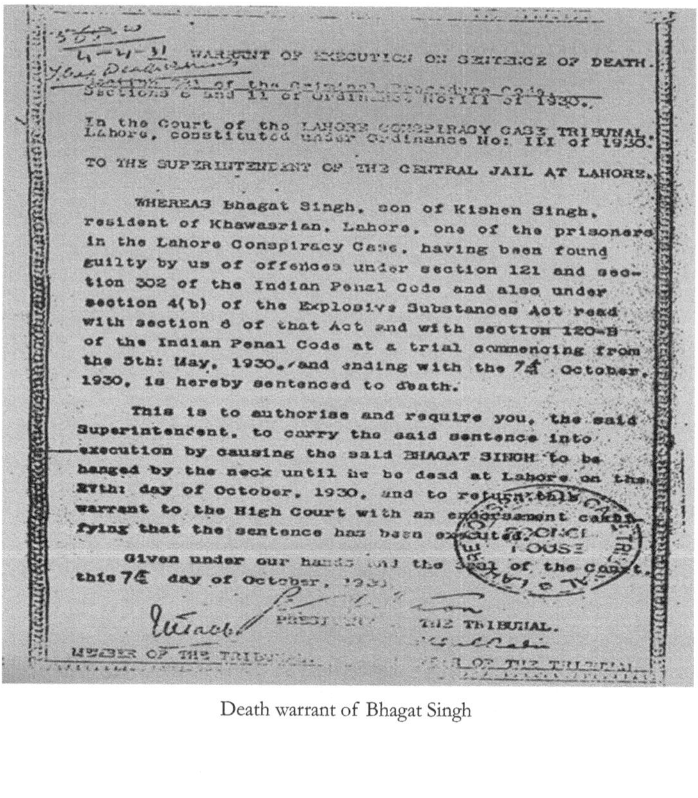

WARRANT OF EXECUTION ON SENTENCE OF DEATH.

~~Section 381 of the Criminal Procedure Code.~~
Sections 6 and 11 of Ordinance No: III of 1930.

In the Court of the LAHORE CONSPIRACY CASE TRIBUNAL, Lahore, constituted under Ordinance No: III of 1930.

TO THE SUPERINTENDENT OF THE CENTRAL JAIL AT LAHORE.

WHEREAS Bhagat Singh, son of Kishen Singh, resident of Khawasrian, Lahore, one of the prisoners in the Lahore Conspiracy Case, having been found guilty by us of offences under section 121 and section 302 of the Indian Penal Code and also under section 4(b) of the Explosive Substances Act read with section 6 of that Act and with section 120-B of the Indian Penal Code at a trial commencing from the 5th: May, 1930, and ending with the 7th October, 1930, is hereby sentenced to death.

This is to authorise and require you, the said Superintendent, to carry the said sentence into execution by causing the said BHAGAT SINGH to be hanged by the neck until he be dead at Lahore on the 27th: day of October, 1930, and to return this warrant to the High Court with an endorsement certifying that the sentence has been executed.

Given under our hands and the seal of the Court this 7th day of October, 1930.

PRESIDENT OF THE TRIBUNAL.

MEMBER OF THE TRIBUNAL. MEMBER OF THE TRIBUNAL.

Death warrant of Bhagat Singh

21.

Letter to B.K. Dutt

This letter gives a glimpse into Bhagat Singh's expectations from his comrades who would escape capital punishment.

Central Jail, Lahore

November, 1930

DEAR BROTHER,

The judgement has been delivered. I am condemned to death. In these cells, besides myself, there are many others prisoners who are waiting to be hanged. The only prayer of these people is that somehow or other they may escape the moose. Perhaps I am the only man amongst them who is anxiously waiting for the day when I will be fortunate enough to embrace the gallows for my ideal.

I will climb the gallows gladly and show to the world as to how bravely the revolutionaries can sacrifice themselves for the cause.

I will be condemned to death, but you are sentenced to transportation for life. You will live and, while living, you will have to show to the world that the revolutionaries not only die for their ideals but can face every calamity. Death should not be a means to escape the worldly difficulties. Those revolutionaries who have by chance escaped the gallows for the ideal but also bear the worst type of tortures in the dark dingy prison cells.

Yours

Bhagat Singh

22.

Letter to Jaidev Gupta

Bhagat Singh wrote this letter to Jaidev Gupta, a close friend from his school days, for some books. It gives an idea of the type of books he used to study in jail. It also shows how keen he was on the intellectual development of his comrades.

Lahore Central Jail

24.7.30

MY DEAR JAIDEV,

Please take following books in my name from Dwarkadas Library and send them through Kulvir on Sunday:

Militarism (Kari Liebknecht) Why Men Fight (B. Russel)

Soviets at Work Collapse of the Second International

Left-Wing Communism Mutual Aid (Prince Kropotkin)

Fields, Factories and Workshops Civil War in France (Marx)

Land Revolution in Russia Spy (Upton Sinclair)

Please send one more book from Punjab Public Library: Historical Materialism (Bukharin). Also, please find out from the librarian if some books have been sent to Borstal Jail. They are facing a terrible famine of books. They had sent a list of books through Sukhdev's brother Jaidev. They have not received any book till now. In case they have no list, then please ask Lala Firoz Chand to send some interesting books of his choice. The books must reach them before I go there on this Sunday. This work is a must. Please keep this in mind.

Also send Punjab Peasants in Prosperity and Debt by Darling and 2 or 3 books of this type for Dr. Alam. Hope you will excuse me for this trouble. I promise I will not trouble you in future. Please remember me to all my friends and convey my respect to Lajjawati. I am sure if Dutt's sister came she will not forget to see me.

With regards

Bhagat Singh

23.

Introduction to Dreamland

Lala Ram Saran Das was convicted for life in 1915 in the first Lahore Conspiracy Case. While in Salem Central Prison, Madras presidency, he wrote a book in verse entitled Dream Land. He passed on his manuscript to Bhagat Singh for an introduction. In this article Bhagat Singh, while appreciating the spirit behind Ram Saran Das's work, criticised his utopian approach to the problems of the revolution. He has also expressed his views on subjects of God, religion, violence and non-violence, spiritualism, literature, poetry, etc.

My noble friend, Ram Saran Das, has asked me to write an introduction to his poetical work, 'The Dreamland'. I am neither a poet nor a literature, neither am I a journalist nor a critic. Hence, by no stretch of imagination can I find the justification of the demand. But the circumstances in which I am placed do not afford any opportunity of discussing the question with the author arguing back and forth, and thereby do not leave me any alternative but to comply with the desire of my friend.

As I am not a poet I am not going to discuss it from that point of view. I have absolutely no knowledge of metre, and do not even know whether judged from metrical standard it would prove correct. Not being a literature I am not going to discuss it with a view of assigning to it its right place in the national literature.

I, being a political worker, can at the utmost discuss it only from that point of view. But here also one factor is making my work practically impossible or at least very difficult. As a rule the introduction is always written by a man who is at one with the author on the contents of the work. But, here the case a quit different. I do not see eye to eye with my friend on all the matters. He was ware of the fact that I differed from him on many vital points. Therefore, may writing is not going to be an introduction at all. It can at the utmost amount to a criticism, and its place will be at the end and not in the beginning of the book.

In the political field 'The Dreamland' occupies a very important place. In the prevailing circumstance it is filling up a very important gap in the movement. As a matter of fact all the political movements of our country that have hitherto played any important role in our modern history, had been lacking the ideal at the achievement of which they aimed. Revolutionary movement is no exception. In spite of all my efforts, I could not find any revolutionary party that had clear ideas as to what they were fighting for, with the exception of the Ghadar Party which, having been inspired by the USA form of government, clearly stated that they wanted to replace the existing government by a Republican form of government. All other parties consisted of men who had but one idea, i.e., to fight against the alien rulers. That idea is quite laudable but cannot be termed a revolutionary idea. We must make it clear that revolution does not merely mean an upheaval or a sanguinary strife. Revolution necessarily implies the programme of systematic reconstruction of society on new and better adapted basis, after complete destruction of the existing state of affairs (i.e., regime).

In the political field the liberals wanted some reform under the present government, while the extremists demanded a bit more and were prepared to employ radical means for the same purpose. Among the revolutionaries, they had always been in favour of extreme methods with one idea, i.e., of overthrow the foreign domination. No doubt, there had been some who were in favour of extorting some reforms through those means. All these movement cannot rightly be designated as revolutionary movement.

But L. Ram Saran Das is the first revolutionary recruited formally in the Punjab by a Bengali absconder in 1908. Since then he had been in touch with the revolutionary movements and finally joined the Ghadar Party but retaining his old ideas that people held about the ideal of their movement. It has another interesting fact to add to its beauty and value. L. Ram Saran Das was sentenced to death in 1915, and the sentence was later on commuted to life transportation. Today, sitting in the condemned cells myself, I can let the readers know as authoritatively that the life imprisonment is comparatively a far harder lot than that of death. L. Ram Saran Das had actually to undergo fourteen years of imprisonment. It was in some southern jail that he wrote this poetry. The then psychology and mental struggle of the author has stamped its impressions upon the poetry and makes it all the more beautiful and interesting. He had been struggling hard against some depressing mood before he had decided to write. In the days when many of his comrades had been let off on undertakings and the temptation had been very strong for everyone and for him, too and when the sweet and painful memories of wife and children had added more to the work. Hence, we find the sudden outburst in the opening paragraph:

"Wife, children, friends that me surround

Were poisonous snakes all around."

He discusses philosophy in the beginning. This philosophy is the backbone of all the revolutionary movement of Bengal as well as of the Punjab. I differ from him on this point very widely. His interpretation of the universe is teleological and metaphysical, which I am a materialist and my interpretation of the phenomenon would be causal. Nevertheless, it is by no means out of place or out of date. The general ideal that are prevailing in our country, are more in accordance with those expressed by him. To fight that depressing mood he resorted to prayers as is evident that the whole of the beginning of the book is devoted to God, His praise, His definition. Belief in God is the outcome of mysticism which is the natural consequence of depression. That this world is 'Maya' or Mithya', a dream or a fiction, is clear mysticism which has been originated and developed by Hindu sages of old ages, such as Shankaracharya and others. But in the materialist philosophy this mode of thinking has got absolutely no place. But this mysticism of the thinking has got absolutely no place. But this mysticism of the author is by no means ignoble or deplorable. It has its own of them are doing very productive labour. The only difference that the socialist society expects is that the mental workers shall no longer be regarded superior to the manual workers shall no longer be regarded superior to the manual workers.

L. Ram Saran Das's idea about free education is really worth considering, and the socialist government has adopted somewhat the same course in Russia.

His discussion about crime is really the most advanced school of thought. Crime is the most serious social problem which needs a very tactful treatment. He has been in jail for the better part of his life. He has got the practical experience. At one place he employs the typical jail terms, 'the light labour, the medium labour and the hard labour', etc. Like all other socialists he suggests that, instead of retribution, i.e., retaliation the reformative theory should form the basis of punishment. Not to punish but to reclaim should be the guiding principle of the administration of justice. Jails should be reformatories and not veritable hells. In this connection the readers should study the Russian prison system.

While dealing with militia he discusses war as well. In my opinion war as an institution shall only occupy a few pages in the Encyclopaedia then, and war materials shall adorn the no conflicting or diverse interests that cause war.

At the utmost we can say that war shall have to be retained as an institution for the transitional period. We can easily understand if we take the example of the present-day Russia. There is the dictatorship of the proletariat at present. They want to establish a socialist society. Meanwhile they have to maintain an army to defend themselves against the capitalist society. But the war-aims would be different. Imperialist designs shall no more actuate our dreamland people to wage wars. There shall be no more war trophies. The revolutionary armies shall march to other lands not to rulers down from their thrones and stop their blood-sucking exploitation and thus to liberate the toiling masses. But, there shall not be the primitive national or racial hatred to goad our men to fight.

World-federation is the most popular and immediate object of all the free thinking people, and the author has well dilated on the subject, and his criticism of the so-called League of Nations is beautiful.

In a footnote under stanza 571 (572) the author touches, though briefly, the question of methods. He says: "Such a kingdom cannot be brought about by physical violent revolutions. It cannot be forced upon society from without. It must grow from within. . . . This can be brought about by the gradual process of Evolution, by educating the masses on the lines mentioned above", etc. This statement does not in itself contain any discrepancy. It is quite correct, but having not been fully explained, is liable to create some misunderstanding, or worse still, a confusion. Does it mean that L. Ram Saran Das has realised the futility of the cult of force? Has he become an orthodox believer in non-violence? No, it does not mean that.

Let me explain what the above quoted statement amounts to. The revolutionaries know better than anybody else that the socialist society cannot be brought about by violent means, but that it should grow and evolve from within. The author suggests education as the only weapon to be employed. But, everybody can easily realise that the present government here, or, as a matter of fact, all the capitalist governments are not only not going to help any such effort, but on the contrary, suppress it mercilessly. Then, what will his 'evolution' achieve? We the revolutionaries are striving to capture power in our hands and to organize a revolutionary government which should employ all its resources for mass education, as is being done in Russia today. After capturing power, peaceful methods shall be employed for constructive work, force shall be employed to crush the obstacles. If that is what the author means, then we are at one. And I am confidant that it is exactly this what he means.

I have discussed the book at great length. I have rather criticised it. But, I am not going to ask any alteration in it, because this has got its historical value. These were the ideas of 1914-15 revolutionaries.

I strongly recommend this book to young men in particular, but with a warning. Please do not read it to follow blindly and take for granted what is written in it. Read it, criticise it, think over it, try to formulate your own ideas with its help.

24.

Regarding Line of Defence in Hari Kishan's Case

On December 23, 1930, when the Governor of Punjab was coming out of the University Hall, Lahore, after deliveringhis convocation address, Hari Kishan fired at him. One man died and the Governor was slightly injured. During the trial, Hari Kishan's defence counsel took the line that Hari Kishan had no intention to kill the Governor and that he only wanted to give a warning.Bhagat Singh was opposed to this line of defence. He wrote to one of his friends outside about how revolutionary cases should be conducted. This letter was published in *The People* in June 1931.

I am very sorry to note that my last letter in this connection did not reach its destination at the proper time and therefore could be of no use, or failed to serve the purpose or which it was written. Hence, I write this letter to let you know my views on the question of defence in the political cases in general and the revolutionary cases in particular. Apart from certain points already discussed in that letter, it shall serve another purpose too, i.e. it shall be a documentary proof that I am not becoming wise after the event.

Anyhow, I wrote in that letter that the plea that the lawyer was suggestion to offer defence, should not be adopted. But it has been done in spite of your, and mine, opposition. Nevertheless, we can now discuss the matter in a better light and can formulate definite Ideas about the future policy regarding defence.

You know that I have never been in favour of defending all the political accused. But this does not imply that the beauty of the real struggle should be altogether spoiled. (Please note that the term beauty is not used in the abstract sense but it means the motive that actuated a particular action). When I say that all the politicals should always defend themselves, I say it with certain reservations. It can be cleared by just one explanation. A man does an act with a certain end in view. After his arrest the political significance of the action should not be diminished. The perpetrator should not become more important than the action itself. Let us further elucidate it with the help of the illustration. Mr. Hari Kishan came to shoot the Governor. I don't want only to discuss the ethical side of the action. I want only to discuss the political side of the case. The man was arrested. Unfortunately, some police official had died in the action. Now comes the question of the defence; well, when fortunately the Governor had escaped there could be a very beautiful statement in his case, i.e., the statement of actual facts as was made in the lower court. And it would have served the legal purpose too. The wisdom and ability of the lawyer depended on his interpretation of the cause of the Sub-Inspector's death. What did he gain by saying that he did not intend to kill the Governor and only wanted to warn him, and all that sort of thing? Can any sensible man imagine even for a moment the possibility of such a design? Had it any legal value? Absolutely none. Then, what was the use of spoiling the beauty of not only the particular action but also the general movement? Warning and futile protests cannot go on forever. The warning has once been given long ago. The revolutionary struggle had begun in right earnest so far as the strength of the revolutionary party allowed. Viceroy's train action was neither a test nor a warning. Similarly, Mr. Hari Kishan's action was part of the struggle itself, not a warning. After the failure of the action, the accused can take it in purely sportman-like spirit. The purpose having been served he ought to have rejoiced in the lucky escape of the Governor. There is no use of killing any one individual. These actions have their political significance in as much as they serve to create a mentality and an atmosphere which shall be very necessary to the final struggle. That is all. Individual actions are to win the moral support of the people. We sometimes designate them as the 'propaganda through deed'.

Now, the people should be defended but subject to the above consideration. This is after all a common principle that all the contending parties always try to gain more and to lose less. No general can ever adopt a policy in which he may have to make a greater sacrifice than the gain expected. Nobody would be more anxious to save the precious life of Mr. Hari Kishan than myself. But I want to let you know that the thing which makes his life precious should by no means be ignored. To save the lives at any cost, is not our policy. It may be the policy of the easy-chair politicians, but it is not ours.

Much of the defence policy depends upon the mentality of the accused himself. But if the accused himself is not only afraid of shrinking but is as enthusiastic as ever, than his work for which he risked his life should be considered first, his personal question afterwards. Again, there may be some sort of confusion. There may be cases where the action is of no general importance in spite of its tremendous local value. There the accused should not be sentimental as to admit the responsibility. The famous trial of Nirmal Kant Rai would be the best illustration.

But in cases like this where it is of such political importance, the personal aspect should not be attached greater value than the political one. If you want to know my frank opinion about his case, let me tell you frankly that it is nothing short of the political murder of an incident of historic importance at the altar o professional (legel) vanity.

Here I may point out one thing more, that the people responsible for this strangulation of the case, having realised their blunder and having become wise after the event in not daring to shoulder their responsibility, are trying to belittle the beauty of the marvellous character of our young comrade. I have heard them saying that Mr. Hari Kishan shirked to face it boldly.

This is a most shame-faced lie. He is the most courageous led I have ever come across. People should have mercy upon us. Better ignored than demoralised and degraded but well looked after.

Lawyers should not be so unscrupulous as to exploit the lives and even deaths of young people who come to sacrifice themselves for so noble a cause as the emancipation of the suffering humanity. I am really . . .Otherwise, why should a lawyer demand such an incredible fee as has been paid in the above case?

In the sedition cases, I may tell you the limit to which we can allow the defence. Last year when one comrade was prosecuted for having delivered a socialistic speech and when he pleaded not guilty to that charge, we were simply astounded. In such cases we should demand the right of free speech. But where such things are attributed to one a he has not said and are contrary to the interests of the movement, deny. Thought in the present movement the Congress has suffered for having allowed its members to go to jail without defending themselves, in my opinion that was a mistake.

Anyhow, I think if you read this letter along with my previous one, you will come to know very clearly my ideas about the defence in political cases. In Mr. Hari Kishan's case, in my opinion, his appeal should be filed in the High Court without fail and every effort should be made to save him.

I hope both these letters indicate everything I want to say on this subject.

25.

To Young Political Workers

Written on February 2, 1931, this document is a sort of behest to young political workers of India. At that time the talk of some sort of compromise between the Congress and the British Government was in the air. Through this document Bhagat Singh explained when a compromise is permissible and when it is not. He also expressed that the way the Congress is conducting the movement, it was bound to end in some sort of compromise. After analysing the prevailing conditions, he finally advised the youth to adopt Marxism as the ideology, work among the people, organize workers and peasants and form the Communist Party.

After Bhagat Singh's execution, this document was published in a mutilated form. All references to the Soviet Union, Marx, Lenin and the Communist Party were carefully deleted. Subsequently, the GOI published it in one of its secret reports in 1936. A photostat copy of the full report is preserved in the library of the Martyrs' Memorial and Freedom Struggle Research Centre at Lucknow.

To The Young Political Workers.

DEAR COMRADES

Our movement is passing through a very important phase at present. After a year's fierce struggle some definite proposals regarding the constitutional reforms have been formulated by the Round Table Conference and the Congress leaders have been invited to give this [Original transcription is unclear — MIA Transcriber]...think it desirable in the present circumstances to call off their movement. Whether they decide in favour or against is a matter of little importance to us. The present movement is bound to end in some sort of compromise. The compromise may be effected sooner or later. And compromise is not such ignoble and deplorable a thing as we generally think. It is rather an indispensable factor in the political strategy. Any nation that rises against the oppressors is bound to fail in the beginning, and to gain partial reforms during the medieval period of its struggle through compromises. And it is only at the last stage — having fully organized all the forces and resources of the nation — that it can possibly strike the final blow in which it might succeed to shatter the ruler's government. But even then it might fail, which makes some sort of compromise inevitable. This can be best illustrated by the Russian example.

In 1905 a revolutionary movement broke out in Russia. All the leaders were very hopeful. Lenin had returned from the foreign countries where he had taken refuge. He was conducting the struggle. People came to tell him that a dozen landlords were killed and a score of their mansions were burnt. Lenin responded by telling them to return and to kill twelve hundred landlords and burn as many of their palaces. In his opinion that would have meant something if revolution failed. Duma was introduced. The same Lenin advocated the view of participating in the Duma. This is what happened in 1907. In 1906 he was opposed to the participation in this first Duma which had granted more scope of work than this second one whose rights had been curtailed. This was due to the changed circumstances. Reaction was gaining the upper hand and Lenin wanted to use the floor of the Duma as a platform to discuss socialist ideas.

Again after the 1917 revolution, when the Bolsheviks were forced to sign the Brest Litovsk Treaty, everyone except Lenin was opposed to it. But Lenin said: "Peace". "Peace and again peace: peace at any cost— even at the cost of many of the Russian provinces to be yielded to German War Lord". When some anti-Bolshevik people condemned Lenin for this treaty, he declared frankly that the Bolsheviks were not in a position to face to German onslaught and they preferred the treaty to the complete annihilation of the Bolshevik Government.

The thing that I wanted to point out was that compromise is an essential weapon which has to be wielded every now and then as the struggle develops. But the thing that we must keep always before us is the idea of the movement. We must always maintain a clear notion as to the aim for the achievement of which we are fighting. That helps us to verify the success and failures of our movements and we can easily formulate the future programme. Tilak's policy, quite apart from the ideal i.e. his strategy, was the best. You are fighting to get sixteen annas from your enemy, you get only one anna. Pocket it and fight for the rest. What we note in the moderates is of their ideal. They start to achieve on anna and they can't get it. The revolutionaries must always keep in mind that they are striving for a complete revolution. Complete mastery of power in their hands. Compromises are dreaded because the conservatives try to disband the revolutionary forces after the compromise from such pitfalls. We must be very careful at such junctures to avoid any sort of confusion of the real issues especially the goal. The British Labour leaders betrayed their real struggle and have been reduced to mere hypocrite imperialists. In my opinion the diehard conservatives are better to us than these polished imperialist Labour leaders. About the tactics and strategy one should study life-work of Lenin. His definite views on the subject of compromise will be found in "Left Wing" Communism.

I have said that the present movement, i.e. the present struggle, is bound to end in some sort of compromise or complete failure.

I said that, because in my opinion, this time the real revolutionary forces have not been invited into the arena. This is a struggle dependent upon the middle class shopkeepers and a few capitalists. Both these, and particularly the latter, can never dare to risk its property or possessions in any struggle. The real revolutionary armies are in the villages and in factories, the peasantry and the labourers. But our bourgeois leaders do not and cannot dare to tackle them. The sleeping lion once awakened from its slumber shall become irresistible even after the achievement of what our leaders aim at. After his first experience with the Ahmedabad labourers in 1920 Mahatma Gandhi declared: "We must not tamper with the labourers. It is dangerous to make political use of the factory proletariat" (The Times, May 1921). Since then, they never dared to approach them. There remains the peasantry. The Bardoli resolution of 1922 clearly denies the horror the leaders felt when they saw the gigantic peasant class rising to shake off not only the domination of an alien nation but also the yoke of the landlords.

It is there that our leaders prefer a surrender to the British than to the peasantry. Leave alone Pt. Jawahar lal. Can you point out any effort to organize the peasants or the labourers? No, they will not run the risk. There they lack. That is why I say they never meant a complete revolution. Through economic and administrative pressure they hoped to get a few more reforms, a few more concessions for the Indian capitalists. That is why I say that this movement is doomed to die, may be after some sort of compromise or even without. They young workers who in all sincerity raise the cry "Long Live Revolution", are not well organized and strong enough to carry the movement themselves. As a matter of fact, even our great leaders, with the exception of perhaps Pt. Motilal Nehru, do not dare to take any responsibility on their shoulders, that is why every now and then they surrender unconditionally before Gandhi. In spite of their differences, they never oppose him seriously and the resolutions have to be carried for the Mahatma.

In these circumstances, let me warn the sincere young workers who seriously mean a revolution, that harder times are coming. Let them beware lest they should get confused or disheartened. After the experience made through two struggles of the Great Gandhi, we are in a better position to form a clear idea of our present position and the future programme.

Now allow me to state the case in the simplest manner. You cry "Long Live Revolution." Let me assume that you really mean it. According to our definition of the term, as stated in our statement in the Assembly Bomb Case, revolution means the complete overthrow of the existing social order and its replacement with the socialist order. For that purpose our immediate aim is the achievement of power. As a matter of fact, the state, the government machinery is just a weapon in the hands of the ruling class to further and safeguard its interest. We want to snatch and handle it to utilise it for the consummation of our ideal, i.e., social reconstruction on new, i.e., Marxist, basis. For this purpose we are fighting to handle the government machinery. All along we have to educate the masses and to create a favourable atmosphere for our social programme. In the struggles we can best train and educate them.

With these things clear before us, i.e., our immediate and ultimate object having been clearly put, we can now proceed with the examination of the present situation. We must always be very candid and quite business-like while analysing any situation. We know that since a hue and cry was raised about the Indians' participation in and share in the responsibility of the Indian government, the Minto-Morley Reforms were introduced, which formed the Viceroy's council with consultation rights only. During the Great War, when the Indian help was needed the most, promises about self-government were made and the existing reforms were introduced. Limited legislative powers have been entrusted to the Assembly but subject to the goodwill of the Viceroy. Now is the third stage.

Now reforms are being discussed and are to be introduced in the near future. How can our young men judge them? This is a question; I do not know by what standard are the Congress leaders going to judge them. But for us, the revolutionaries, we can have the following criteria:

1. Extent of responsibility transferred to the shoulders of the Indians.

2. From of the Government institutions that are going to be introduced and the extent of the right of participation given to the masses.

3. Future prospects and the safeguards.

These might require a little further elucidation. In the first place, we can easily judge the extent of responsibility given to our people by the control our representatives will have on the executive. Up till now, the executive was never made responsible to the Legislative Assembly and the Viceroy had the veto power, which rendered all the efforts of the elected members futile. Thanks to the efforts of the Swaraj Party, the Viceroy was forced every now and then to use these extraordinary powers to shamelessly trample the solemn decisions of the national representatives under foot. It is already too well known to need further discussion.

Now in the first place we must see the method of the executive formation: Whether the executive is to be elected by the members of a popular assembly or is to be imposed from above as before, and further, whether it shall be responsible to the house or shall absolutely affront it as in the past?

As regards the second item, we can judge it through the scope of franchise. The property qualifications making a man eligible to vote should be altogether abolished and universal suffrage be introduced instead. Every adult, both male and female, should have the right to vote. At present we can simply see how far the franchise has been extended.

I may here make a mention about provincial autonomy. But from whatever I have heard, I can only say that the Governor imposed from above, equipped with extraordinary powers, higher and above the legislative, shall prove to be no less than a despot. Let us better call it the "provincial tyranny" instead of "autonomy." This is a strange type of democratisation of the state institutions.

The third item is quite clear. During the last two years the British politicians have been trying to undo Montague's promise for another dole of reforms to be bestowed every ten years till the British Treasury exhausts.

We can see what they have decided about the future.

Let me make it clear that we do not analyse these things to rejoice over the achievement, but to form a clear idea about our situation, so that we may enlighten the masses and prepare them for further struggle. For us, compromise never means surrender, but a step forward and some rest. That is all and nothing else.

Having discussed the present situation, let us proceed to discuss the future programme and the line of action we ought to adopt. As I have already stated, for any revolutionary party a definite programme is very essential. For, you must know that revolution means action. It means a change brought about deliberately by an organized and systematic work, as opposed to sudden and unorganised or spontaneous change or breakdown. And for the formulation of a programme, one must necessarily study:

1. The goal.

2. The premises from where were to start, i.e., the existing conditions.

3. The course of action, i.e., the means and methods.

Unless one has a clear notion about these three factors, one cannot discuss anything about programme.

We have discussed the present situation to some extent. The goal also has been slightly touched. We want a socialist revolution, the indispensable preliminary to which is the political revolution. That is what we want. The political revolution does not mean the transfer of state (or more crudely, the power) from the hands of the British to the Indian, but to those Indians who are at one with us as to the final goal, or to be more precise, the power to be transferred to the revolutionary party through popular support. After that, to proceed in right earnest is to organize the reconstruction of the whole society on the socialist basis. If you do not mean this revolution, then please have mercy. Stop shouting "Long Live Revolution." The term revolution is too sacred, at least to us, to be so lightly used or misused. But if you say you are for the national revolution and the aims of your struggle is an Indian republic of the type of the United State of America, then I ask you to please let known on what forces you rely that will help you bring about that revolution. Whether national or the socialist, are the peasantry and the labour. Congress leaders do not dare to organize those forces. You have seen it in this movement. They know it better than anybody else that without these forces they are absolutely helpless. When they passed the resolution of complete independence — that really meant a revolution — they did not mean it. They had to do it under pressure of the younger element, and then they wanted to us it as a threat to achieve their hearts' desire — Dominion Status. You can easily judge it by studying the resolutions of the last three sessions of the Congress. I mean Madras, Calcutta and Lahore. At Calcutta, they passed a resolution asking for Dominion Status within twelve months, otherwise they would be forced to adopt complete independence as their object, and in all solemnity waited for some such gift till midnight after the 31st December, 1929. Then they found themselves "honour bound" to adopt the Independence resolution, otherwise they did not mean it. But even then Mahatmaji made no secret of the fact that the door (for compromise) was open. That was the real spirit. At the very outset they knew that their movement could not but end in some compromise. It is this half-heartedness that we hate, not the compromise at a particular stage in the struggle. Anyway, we were discussing the forces on which you can depend for a revolution. But if you say that you will approach the peasants and labourers to enlist their active support, let me tell you that they are not going to be fooled by any sentimental talk. They ask you quite candidly: what are they going to gain by your revolution for which you demand their sacrifices, what difference does it make to them whether Lord Reading is the head of the Indian government or Sir Purshotamdas Thakordas? What difference for a peasant if Sir Tej Bahadur Sapru replaces Lord Irwin! It is useless to appeal to his national sentiment. You can't "use" him for your purpose; you shall have to mean seriously and to make him understand that the revolution is going to be his and for his good. The revolution of the proletariat and for the proletariat.

When you have formulated this clear-cut idea about your goals you can proceed in right earnest to organize your forces for such an action. Now there are two different phases through which you shall have to pass. First, the preparation; second, the action.

After the present movement ends, you will find disgust and some disappointment amongst the sincere revolutionary workers. But you need not worry. Leave sentimentalism aside. Be prepared to face the facts. Revolution is a very difficult task. It is beyond the power of any man to make a revolution. Neither can it be brought about on any appointed date. It is brought can it be brought about on an appointed date. It is brought about by special environments, social and economic. The function of an organized party is to utilise an such opportunity offered by these circumstances. And to prepare the masses and organize the forces for the revolution is a very difficult task. And that required a very great sacrifice on the part of the revolutionary workers. Let me make it clear that if you are a businessman or an established worldly or family man, please don't play with fire. As a leader you are of no use to the party. We have already very many such leaders who spare some evening hours for delivering speeches. They are useless. We require — to use the term so dear to Lenin — the "professional revolutionaries". The whole-time workers who have no other ambitions or life-work except the revolution. The greater the number of such workers organized into a party, the great the chances of your success.

To proceed systematically, what you need the most is a party with workers of the type discussed above with clear-cut ideas and keen perception and ability of initiative and quick decisions. The party shall have iron discipline and it need not necessarily be an underground party, rather the contrary. Thought the policy of voluntarily going to jail should altogether be abandoned. That will create a number of workers who shall be forced to lead an underground life. They should carry on the work with the same zeal. And it is this group of workers that shall produce worthy leaders for the real opportunity.

The party requires workers which can be recruited only through the youth movement. Hence we find the youth movement as the starting point of our programme. The youth movement should organize study circles, class lectures and publication of leaflets, pamphlets, books and periodicals. This is the best recruiting and training ground for political workers.

Those young men who may have matured their ideas and may find themselves ready to devote their life to the cause, may be transferred to the party. The party workers shall always guide and control the work of the youth movement as well. The party should start with the work of mass propaganda. It is very essential. One of the fundamental causes of the failure of the efforts of the Ghadar Party (1914-15) was the ignorance, apathy and sometimes active opposition of the masses. And apart from that, it is essential for gaining the active sympathy of and of and organising the peasants and workers. The name of party or rather, a communist party. This party of political workers, bound by strict discipline, should handle all other movements. It shall have to organize the peasants' and workers' parties, labour unions, and kindred political bodies. And in order to create political consciousness, not only of national politics but class politics as well, the party should organize a big publishing campaign. Subjects on all proletens enlightening the masses of the socialist theory shall be within easy reach and distributed widely. The writings should be simple and clear.

There are certain people in the labour movement who enlist some absurd ideas about the economic liberty of the peasants and workers without political freedom. They are demagogues or muddle-headed people. Such ideas are unimaginable and preposterous. We mean the economic liberty of the masses, and for that very purpose we are striving to win the political power. No doubt in the beginning, we shall have to fight for little economic demands and privileges of these classes. But these struggles are the best means for educating them for a final struggles are the best means for educating them for a final struggle to conquer political power.

Apart from these, there shall necessarily be organized a military department. This is very important. At times its need is felt very badly. But at that time you cannot start and formulate such a group with substantial means to act effectively. Perhaps this is the topic that needs a careful explanation. There is very great probability of my being misunderstood on this subject. Apparently I have acted like a terrorist. But I am not a terrorist. I am a revolutionary who has got such definite ideas of a lengthy programme as is being discussed here. My "comrades in arms" might accuse me, like Ram Prasad Bismil, for having been subjected to certain sort of reaction in the condemned cell, which is not true. I have got the same ideas, same convictions, same convictions, same zeal and same spirit as I used to have outside, perhaps — nay, decidedly — better. Hence I warn my readers to be careful while reading my words. They should not try to read anything between the lines. Let me announce with all the strength at my command, that I am not a terrorist and I never was, expected perhaps in the beginning of my revolutionary career. And I am convinced that we cannot gain anything through those methods. One can easily judge it from the history of the Hindustan Socialist Republican Association. All our activities were directed towards an aim, i.e., identifying ourselves with the great movement as its military wing. If anybody has misunderstood me, let him amend his ideas. I do not mean that bombs and pistols are useless, rather the contrary. But I mean to say that mere bomb-throwing is not only useless but sometimes harmful. The military department of the party should always keep ready all the war-material it can command for any emergency. It should back the political work of the party. It cannot and should not work independently.

On these lines indicated above, the party should proceed with its work. Through periodical meetings and conferences they should go on educating and enlightening their workers on all topics. If you start the work on these lines, you shall have to be very sober. The programme requires at least twenty years for its fulfillment. Cast aside the youthful dreams of a revolution within ten years of Gandhi's utopian promises of Swaraj in One Year. It requires neither the emotion nor the death, but the life of constant struggle, suffering and sacrifice. Crush your individuality first. Shake off the dreams of personal comfort. Then start to work. Inch by inch you shall have to proceed. It needs courage, perseverance and very strong determination. No difficulties and no hardships shall discourage you. No failure and betrayals shall dishearten you. No travails imposed upon you shall snuff out the revolutionary will in you. Through the ordeal of sufferings and sacrifice you shall come out victorious. And these individual victories shall be the valuable assets of the revolution.

LONG LIVE REVOLUTION

2nd February, 1931

26.

Why I am an Atheist

Bhagat Singh wrote this article in reply to a remark given by Baba Randhir Singh, a freedom fighter, who was in Lahore Central Jail during 1930-31. Randhir Singh was a God-fearing religious man. It pained him to learn that Bhagat Singh was a non-believer. He somehow managed to see Bhagat Singh in the condemned cell and tried to convince him about the existence of God, but failed. Baba lost his temper and said tauntingly: "You are giddy with fame and have developed an ego which is standing like a black curtain between you and the God." It was in reply to this that Bhagat Singh wrote this important and thought-provoking article.

A new question has cropped up. Is it due to vanity that I do not believe in the existence of an omnipotent, omnipresent and omniscient God? I had never imagined that I would ever have to confront such a question. But conversation with some friends has given me a hint that certain of my friends– if I am not claiming too much in thinking them to be so– are inclined to conclude from the brief contact they have had with me, that it was too much on my part to deny the existence of God and that there was a certain amount of vanity that actuated my disbelief. Well, the problem is a serious one. I do not boast to be quite above these human traits. I am a man and nothing more. None can claim to be more. I also have this weakness in me. Vanity does form a part of my nature. Amongst my comrades I was called an autocrat. Even my friend Mr. B.K. Dutt sometimes called me so. On certain occasions I was decried as a despot. Some friends do complain, and very seriously too, that involuntarily thrust my opinions upon others and get my proposals accepted. That this is true up to a certain extent, I do not deny. This may amount to egotism. There is vanity in me inasmuch as our cult as opposed to other popular creeds is concerned. But that is not personal. It may be, it is only legitimate pride in our cult and does not amount to vanity. Vanity, or to be more precise "Ahankar", is the excess of undue pride in one's self. Whether it is such an undue pride that has led me to atheism or whether it is after very careful study of the subject and after much consideration that I have come to disbelieve in God, is a question that I intend to discuss here. Let me first make it clear that egotism and vanity are two different things.

In the first place, I have altogether failed to comprehend as to how undue pride or vaingloriousness could ever stand in the way of a man in believing in God. I can refuse to recognise the greatness of a really great man, provided I have also achieved a certain amount of popularity without deserving it or without having possessed the qualities really essential or indispensable for the same purpose. That much is conceivable. But in what way can a man believing in God cease believing due to his personal vanity? There are only two ways. The man should either begin to think himself a rival of God or he may begin to believe himself to be God. In neither case can he become a genuine atheist. In the first case he does not even deny the existence of his rival. In the second case as well, he admits the existence of a conscious being behind the screen guiding all the movements of nature. It is of no importance to us whether he thinks himself to be that supreme being or whether he thinks the supreme being or whether he thinks the supreme conscious being to be somebody apart from him means an atheist. Well, here I am. I neither belong to the first category nor to the second. I deny the very existence of that Almighty Supreme Being. Why I deny it, shall be dealt with later on. Here I want to clear one thing, that it is not vanity that has actuated me to adopt the doctrines of atheism. I am neither a rival a rival nor an incarnation, nor the Supreme Being Himself. One point is decided, that it is not vanity that has led me to this mode of thinking. Let me examine the facts to disprove this allegation. According to these friends of mine I have grown vainglorious perhaps due to the undue popularity gained during the trials - both Delhi Bomb and Lahore Conspiracy Cases. Well, let us see if their premises are correct. My atheism is not of so recent origin. I had stopped believing in God when I was an obscure young man, of whose existence my above-mentioned friends were not even aware. At least a college student cannot cherish any short of undue pride which may lead him to atheism. Thought a favourite with some professors and disliked by certain others. I was never an industrious or a studious boy. I could not get any chance of indulging in such feelings as vanity. I was rather a boy with a very shy nature, who had certain pessimistic dispositions about the future career. And in those days, I was not a perfect atheist. My grandfather under whose influence I was brought up is an orthodox Arya Samajist. An Arya Samajist is anything but an atheist. After finishing my primary education I joined the D.A.V. School of Lahore and stayed in its Boarding House for full one year. There, apart from morning and evening prayers, I used to recite "Gayatri Mantra" for hours and hours. I was perfect devotee in those days. Later on I began to live with my father. He is a liberalinas much as the orthodoxy of religions is concerned. It was through his teachings that I aspired to devote my life to the cause of freedom. But he is not an atheist. He is a firm believer. He used to encourage me for offering prayers daily. So this how I was brought up. In the Non-Cooperation days I joined the National College. It was there that I began to think liberally and discuss and criticise all the religious problem, even about God. But still I was a devout believer. By that time I had begun to preserve the unshorn and unclipped long hair but I could never believe in the mythology and doctrines of Sikhism or any other religion. But I had a firm faith in God's existence.

Later on I joined the revolutionary party. The first leader with whom I came in contact, though not convinced, could not dare to deny the existence of God. On my persistent inquiries about God, he used to say: "Pray whenever you want to." Now this is atheism less courage required for the adoption of that creed. The second leader with whom I came in contact was a firm believer. Let me mention his name-respected Comrade Shachindra Nath Sanyal, now undergoing life transportation in connection with the Kakori Conspiracy Case. From the very first page of his famous and only book, Bandi Jivan (or Incarcerated Life), the Glory of God is sung vehemently. On the last page of the second part of that beautiful book, his mystic-because of vedantism-praises showered upon God form a very conspicuous part of his thoughts. "The Revolutionary" distributed throughout India on January 28th, 1925, was according to the prosecution story the result of his intellectual labour. Now, as is inevitable in the secret work the prominent leader expresses his own views which are very dear to his person, and the rest of the workers have to acquiesce in them, in spite of differences which they might have. In that leaflet one full paragraph was devoted to praise the Almighty and His rejoicings and doing. That is all mysticism. What I wanted to point out was that the idea of disbelief had not even germinated in the revolutionary party. The famous Kakori martyrs-all four of them-passed their last days in prayers. Ram Prasad Bismil was an orthodox Arya Samajist. Despite his wide studies in the field of socialism and communism, Rajen Lahiri could not suppress his desire of reciting hymns of the Upanishads and the Gita. I saw only one man amongst them, who never prayed and used to say: "Philosophy is the outcome of human weakness or limitation of knowledge." He is also undergoing a sentence of transportation for life. But he also never dared to deny the existence of God.

Up to that period I was only a romantic idealist revolutionary. Up till then we were to follow. Now come the time to shoulder the whole responsibility. Due to the inevitable reaction for some time the very existence of the party seemed impossible. Enthusiastic comrades - nay, leaders-began to jeer at us. For some time I was afraid that some day I also might not be convinced of the futility of our own programme. That was a turning point in my revolutionary career. "Study" was the cry that reverberated in the corridors of my mind. Study to enable yourself with arguments in favour of your cult. I began to study. My previous faith and convictions underwent methods alone which was so prominent amongst our predecessors, was replaced by serious ideas. No more mysticism, no more blind faith. Realism became our cult. Use of force justifiable when resorted to as a matter of terrible necessity: nonviolence as policy indispensable for all mass movements. So much about methods. The most important thing was the clear conception of the ideal for which we were to fight. As there were no important activities in the field of action I got ample opportunity to study various ideals of the world revolution. I studied Bakunin, the anarchist leader, something of Marx, the father of communism, and much of Lenin, Trotsky and others-the men who had successfully carried out a revolution in their country. They were all atheists. Bakunin's God and State, though only fragmentary, is an interesting study of the subject. Later still I came across a book entitled Common Sense by Nirlamba Swami, It was only a sort of mystic atheism. This subject became of utmost interest to me. By the end of 1926 I had been convinced as to the baselessness of the theory of existence of an almighty supreme being who created, guided and controlled the universe. I had given out this disbelief of mine. I began discussion on the subjects with my friends. I had become a pronounced atheist. But what it meant will presently be discussed.

In May 1927 I was arrested at Lahore. The arrest was a surprise. I was quite unaware of the fact that the police wanted me. All of a sudden, while passing through a garden, I found myself surrounded by police. To my own surprise, I was very calm at that time. I did not feel any sensation, nor did I experience any excitement. I was taken into police custody. Next day I was taken to the Railway Police lock-up where I was to pass full one month. After many day's conversation with the police officials I guessed that they had some information regarding my connection with the Kakori party and my other activities in connection with the revolutionary movement. They told me that I had been to Lucknow while the trial was going on there, that I had negotiated a certain scheme about their rescue, that the after obtaining their approval, we had procured some bombs, that by way of test one of the bombs was thrown in the crowd on the occasion of Dussehra 1926. They further informed me, in my interest, that if I could give any statement throwing some light on the activities of the revolutionary party, I was not to be imprisoned but on the contrary set free and rewarded, even without being produced as an approver in the court. I laughed at the proposal. It was all humbug. People holding ideas like ours do not throw bombs on their on innocent people. One fine morning Mr. Newman, the then Senior Superintendent of C.I.D., came to me. And after much sympathetic talk with me, imparted– to him the extremely sad– news that if I did not give any statement as demanded by them, they would be forced to send me up for trial for conspiracy to wage war in connection with Kakari Case and for brutal murders in connection with Dussehra bomb outrage. And he further informed me that they had evidence enough to get me convicted and hanged. In those day I believed– though I was quite innocent–the police could do it if they desired. That very day certain police officials began to persuade me to offer my prayers to God regularly, both the times. Now I was an atheist. I wanted to settle for myself whether it was in the days of peace and enjoyment alone that I could boast of being an atheistor whether during such hard times as well, I could stick to those principles of mine. After great consideration I decided that I could not lead myself to believe in and pray to God. No, I never did. That was the real test and I came out successful. Never for a moment did I desire to save my neck at the cost of certain other things. So I was a staunch disbeliever; and have ever since been. It was not an easy job to stand that test. 'Belief' softens the hardships, even can make them pleasant. In God man can find very strong consolation and support. Without Him man has to depend upon himself. To stand upon one's own legs amid storms and hurricanes is not a child's play. At such testing moments, vanity–if–any–evaporates and man cannot dare to defy the general beliefs. If he does, then we must conclude that he has got certain other strength than mere vanity. This is exactly the situation now.

Judgement is already too well known. Within a week it is to be pronounced. What is the consolation with the exception of the idea that I am going to sacrifice my life for a cause? A God-believing Hindu might be expecting to be reborn as a king, a Muslim or a Christian might dream of the luxuries to be enjoyed in paradise and the reward he is to get for his suffering and sacrifices. But, what am I to expect? I know the moment under my feet, that will be the final moment-that will be the last moment. I, or to be more precise, my soul as interpreted in the metaphysical terminology shall all be finished there. Nothing further. A short life of struggle with no such magnificent end, shall in itself be the reward, if I have the courage to take it in that light. That is all. With no selfish motive or desire to be awarded here or hereafter, quite disinterestedly, have I devoted my life to the cause of independence, because I could not do otherwise. The day we find a great number of men and women with this psychology, who cannot devote themselves to anything else than the service of mankind and emancipation of the suffering humanity, that day shall inaugurate the era of liberty. Not to become a king, nor to gain any other rewards here, or in the next birth or after death in paradise, shall they be inspired to challenge the oppressors, exploiters, and tyrants, but to cast off the yoke of serfdom from the neck of humanity and to establish liberty and peace shall they tread this-to their individual selves perilous and to their noble selves the only glorious imaginable-path. Is the pride in their noble cause to be misinterpreted as vanity? Who dares to utter such an abominable epithet? To him I say either he is a fool or a knave. Let us forgive him for he cannot realise the depth, the emotion, the sentiment and the noble feelings that surge in that heart. His heart is dead as a mere lump of flesh, his eyes are weak, the evils of other interests having been cast over them. Self-reliance is always liable to be interpreted as vanity. It is sad and miserable but there is no help.

You go and oppose the prevailing faith, you go and criticise a hero, a great man who is generally believed to be above criticism because he his thought to be infallible, the strength of your argument shall force the multitude to decry you as vainglorious. This is due to the mental stagnation. Criticism and independent thinking are the two indispensable qualities of a revolutionary. Because Mahatamaji is great, therefore none should criticise him. Because he has risen above, therefore everything he says-may be in the field of Politics or Religion, Economics or Ethics-is right. Whether you are convinced or not you must say: "Yes, that's true". This mentality does not lead towards progress. It is rather too obviously reactionary.

Because our forefathers had set up a faith in some supreme being-the Almighty God-therefore, any man who dares to challenge the validity of that faith, or the very existence of that supreme being, he shall have to be called an apostate, a renegade. If his argument are too sound to be refuted by counter-arguments and spirit too strong to be cowed down by the threat of misfortunes that may befall him by the wrath of the Almighty, he shall be decried as vainglorious, his spirit to be denominated as vanity. Then, why do waste time in this vain discussion? Why try to argue out the whole thing? This question is coming before the public for the first time, and is being handled in this matter of fact way for the first time, hence this lengthy discussion.

As for the first question, I think I have cleared that it is not vanity that has led me to atheism. My way of argument has proved to be convincing or not, that is to be judged by my readers, not me. I know in the present circumstances my faith in God would have made my life easier, my burden lighter, and my disbelief in Him has turned all the circumstances too dry, and the situation may assume too harsh a shape. A little bit of mysticism can make it poetical. But I do not want the help of any intoxication to meet my fate. I am a realist. I have been trying to overpower the instinct in me by the help of reason. I have not always been successful in achieving this end. But man's duty is to try and endeavour, success depends upon chance and environments.

As for the second question that if it was not vanity, then there ought to be some reason to disbelieve the old and still prevailing faith of the existence of God. Yes, I come to that now. Reason there is. According to me, any man who has got some reasoning power at his command always tries to reason out his environments. Where direct proofs are lacking philosophy occupies the important place. As I have already stated, a certain revolutionary friend used to say that philosophy is the outcome of human weakness. When our ancestors had leisure enough to try to solve out the mystery of this world, its past, present and the future, its whys and wherefores, they having been terribly short of direct proofs, everybody tried to solve the problem in his own way. Hence we find the wide differences in the fundamentals of various religious creeds, which sometimes assume very antagonistic and conflicting shapes. Not only the Oriental and Occidental philosophies differ, there are differences even amongst various schools of thought in each hemisphere. Amongst Oriental religions, the Moslem faith is not at all compatible with

Hindu faith. In India alone Buddhism and Jainism are sometimes quite separate from Brahmanism, in which there are again conflicting faiths as Arya Samaj and Sanatan Dharma. Charwak is still another independent thinker of the past ages. He challenged the authority of God in the old times. All these creeds differ from each other on the fundamental question; and everybody considers himself to be on the right. There lies the misfortune. Instead of using the experiments and expressions of the ancient Savants and thinkers as a basis for our future struggle against ignorance and to try to find out a solution to this mysterious problem, we lathargical as we have proved to be, raise the hue and cry of faith, unflinching and unwavering faith to their versions and thus are guilty of stagnation in human progress.

Any man who stands for progress has to criticise, disbelieve and challenge every item of the old faith. Item by item he has to reason out every nook and corner of the prevailing faith. If after considerable reasoning one is led to believe in any theory or philosophy, his faith is welcomed. His reasoning can be mistaken, wrong, misled, and sometimes fallacious. But he is liable to correction because reason is the guiding star of his life. But mere faith and blind faith is dangerous: it dulls the brain, and makes a man reactionary. A man who claims to be a realist has to challenge the whole of the ancient faith. If it does not stand the onslaught of reason it crumbles down. Then the first thing for him is to shatter the whole down and clear a space for the erection of a new philosophy. This is the negative side. After it begins the positive work in which sometimes some material of the old faith may be used for the purpose of reconstruction. As far as I am concerned, let me admit at the very outset that I have not been able to study much on this point. I had a great desire to study the Oriental philosophy but I could not get any chance or opportunity to do the same. But so far as the negative study is under discussion, I think I am convinced to the extent of questioning the soundness of the old faith. I have been convinced as to non-existence of a conscious supreme being who is guiding and directing the movements of nature. We believe in nature and the whole progressive movement aims at the domination of man over nature for his service. There is no conscious power behind it to direct. This is what our philosophy is.

As for the negative side, we ask a few question from the 'believers'.

(1) If, as you believe, there is an almighty, omnipresent, omniscient and omnipotent God, who created the earth or world, please let me know why did

he create it? This world of woes and miseries, a veritable, eternal combination of number-less tragedies: Not a single soul being perfectly satisfied.

Pray, don't say that it is His Law. If he is bound by any law, he is not omnipotent. He is another slave like ourselves. Please don't say that it is his enjoyment. Nero burnt one Rome. He killed a very limited number of people. He created very few tragedies, all to his perfect enjoyment. And, what is his place in History? By what names do the historians mention him? All the venomous epithets are showered upon him. Pages are blackened with invective diatribes condemning Nero, the tyrant, the heartless, the wicked. One Changexkhan sacrificed a few thousand lives to seek pleasure in it and we hate the very name. Then, how are you going to justify your almighty, eternal Nero, who has been, and is still causing numberless tragedies every day, every hour and every minute? How do you think to support his misdoings which surpass those of Changez every single moment? I say why did he create this world - a veritable hell, a place of constant and bitter unrest? Why did the Almighty create man when he had the power not to do it? What is the justification for all this? Do you say, to award the innocent sufferers hereafter and to punish the wrongdoers as well? Well, well: How far shall you justify a man who may dare to inflict wounds upon your body to apply a very soft and soothing ointment upon it afterwards? How far the supporters and organisers of the Gladiator institution were justified in throwing men before the half-starved furious lions to be cared for and well locked after if they could survive and could manage to escape death by the wild beasts? That is why I ask: Why did the conscious supreme being create this world and man in it? To seek pleasure? Where, then, is the difference between him and Nero?

You Mohammadans and Christians: Hindu philosophy shall still linger on to offer another argument. I ask you, what is your answer to the above-mentioned question? You don't believe in previous birth. Like Hindus, you cannot advance the argument of previous misdoings of the apparently quite innocent suffers. I ask you, why did the omnipotent labour for six days to create the world through word and each day to say that all was well? Call him today. Show him the past history. Make him study the present situation. Let us see if he dares to say: "All is well."

From the dungeons of prisons, from the stores of starvation consuming millions upon millions of human beings in slums and huts, from the exploited labourers, patiently or say apathetically watching the procedure of their blood being sucked by the capitalist vampires, and the wastage of human energy that will make a man with the least common sense shiver with horror, and from the preference of throwing the surplus of production in oceans rather than to distribute amongst the needy producers - to the palaces of kings built upon the foundation laid with human bones. . . . let him see all this and let him say: "All is well." Why and wherefore? That is my question. You are silent. Alright then, I proceed.

Well, you Hindus, you say all the present sufferers belong to the class of sinners of the previous births. Good. You say the present oppressors were saintly people in their previous births, hence they enjoy power. Let me admit that your ancestors were very shrewd people, they tried to find out theories strong enough to hammer down all the efforts of reason and disbelief. But let us analyse how for this argument can really stand.

From the point of view of the most famous jurists, punishment can be justified only from three or four ends, to meet which it is inflicted upon the wrongdoer. They are retributive, reformative and deterrent. The retributive theory is now being condemned by all the advanced thinkers. Deterrent theory is also following the same fate. Reformative theory is the only one which is essential and indispensable for human progress. It aims at returning the offender as a most competent and a peace-loving citizen to the society. But, what is the nature of punishment inflicted by God upon men, even if we suppose them to be offenders? You say he sends them to be born as a punishments to be 84 lakhs. I ask you: what is its reformative effect upon man? How many men have met you who say that they were born as a donkey in previons birth for having committed any sin? None. Don't quote your Puranas. I have noscope to touch your mythologies. Moreover, do you know that the greatest sin in this world is to be poor? Poverty is a sin, it is a punishment. I ask you how far would you appreciate a criminologist, a jurist or a legislator who proposes such measures of punishment which shall inevitably force men to commit more offences? Had not your God thought of this, or he also had to learn these things by experience, but at the cost of untold sufferings to be borne by humanity? What do you think shall be the fate of a man who has been born in a poor and illiterate family of, say, a chamar or a sweeper? He is poor hence he cannot study. He is hated and shunned by his fellow human beings who think themselves to be his superiors having been born in, say, a higher caste. His ignorance, his heart towards society. Suppose he commits a sin, who shall bear the consequences? God, he or the learned ones of the society? What about the punishment of those people who were deliberately kept ignorant by the haughty and egotist Brahmans, and who had to pay the penalty by bearing the stream of being let (not lead) in their ears for having heard a few sentences of your Sacred Books of learning - the Vedas? If they committed any offence, who was to be responsible for them and who was to inventions of the privileged ones; they justify their usurped power, riches and superiority by the help of these theories. Yes, it was perhaps Upton Sinclair that wrote at some place that just make a man a believer in immortality and then rob him of all his riches and possessions. He shall help you even in that ungrudgingly. The coalition among the religious preachers and possessors of power brought forth jails, gallown, knouts and these theories.

I ask why your omnipotent God does not stop every man when he is committing any sin or offence? He can do it quite easily. Why did he not kill warlords or kill the fury of war in them and thus avoid the catastrophe hurled down on the head of humanity by the Great War? Why does he not just produce a certain sentiment in the mind of the British people to liberate India? Why does he not infuse the altruistic enthusiasm in the hearts of all capitalists to forego their rights of personal possessions of means of production and thus redeem the whole labouring community, nay, the whole human society, from the bondage of capitalism? You want to reason out the practicability of socialist theory, I leave it for your almighty to enforce it. People recognise the merits of socialism inasmuch as the general welfare is concerned. They oppose it under the pretext of its being impracticable. Let the Almighty step in and arrange everything in an orderly fashion. Now don't try to advance round about arguments, they are out of order. Let me tell you, British rule is here not because God wills it, but because they possess power and we do not dare to oppose them. Not that it is with the help of God that they are keeping us under their subjection, but it is with the help of guns and rifles, bomb and bullets, police and militia, and our apathy, that they are successfully committing the most deplorable sin against society - the outrageous exploitation of one nation by another. Where is God? What is he doing? Is he enjoying all these woes of human race? A Nero, a Changez: Down with him.

Do you ask me how I explain the origin of this world and origin of man? Alright, I tell you, Charles Darwin has tried to throw some light on the subject. Study him. Read Soham Swami's Common Sense. It shall answer your question to some extent. This is a phenomenon of nature. The accidental mixture of different substances in the shape of nebulae produced this earth. When? Consult history. The same process produced animals and, in the long run, man. Read Darwin's Origin of Species. And all telater progress is due to man's constant conflict with nature and his efforts to override it. This is the briefest possible explanation of the phenomenon.

Your other argument may be just to ask why a child is born blind or lame if not due to his deeds committed in the previous birth? This problem has been explained away by biologists as a mere biological phenomenon. According to them the whole burden rests upon the shoulders of the parents who may be conscious or ignorant of their own deeds which led to mutilation of the child previous to its birth.

Naturally, you may ask another question, though it is quite childish in essence. If no god existed, how did the people come to believe in him? My answer is clear and brief. As they came to believe in ghosts and evil spirits; the only difference is that belief in God is almost universal and the philosophy well developed. Unlike certain of the radicals I would not attribute its origin to the ingenuity of the exploiters who wanted to keep the people under their subjection by preaching the existence of a supreme being and then claiming an authority and sanction from him for their privileged positions, though I do not differ with them on the essential point that all faiths, religions, creeds and such other institutions became in turn the mere supporters of the tyrannical and exploiting institutions, men and classes. Rebellion against king is always a sin, according to every religion.

As regards the origin of God, my own idea is that having realised the limitation of man, his weaknesses and shortcoming having been taken into consideration, God was brought into imaginary existence to encourage man to face boldly all the trying circumstances, to meet all dangers manfully and to check and restrain his outbursts in prosperity and affluence. God, both will his private laws and parental generosity, was imagined and painted in greater details. He was to serve as a deterrent factor when his fury and private laws were discussed, so that man may not become a danger to society. He was to serve as a father, mother, sister and brother, friend and helper, when his parental qualifications were to be explained. So that when man be in great distress, having been betrayed and deserted by all friends, he may find consolation in the idea that an ever-true friend, was still there to help him, to support him and that he was almighty and could do anything. Really that was useful to the society in the primitive age. The idea of God is helpful to man in distress.

Society has to fight out this belief as well as was fought the idol worship and the narrow conception of religion. Similarly, when man tries to stand on his own legs and become a realist, he shall have to throw the faith aside, and to face manfully all the distress, trouble, in which the circumstances may throw him. That is exactly my state of affairs. It is not my vanity, my friends. It is my mode of thinking that has made me an atheist. I don't know whether in my case belief in God and offering of daily prayers which I consider to be most selfish and degraded act on the part of man, whether these prayers can prove to be helpful or they shall make my case worse still. I have read of atheists facing all troubles quite boldly; so am I trying to stand like a man with an erect head to the last, even on the gallows.

Let us see how I carry on. One friend asked me to pray. When informed of my atheism, he said: "During your last days you will begin to believe." I said: "No, dear Sir, it shall not be. I will think that to be an act of degradation and demoralisation on my part. For selfish motives I am not going to pray." Readers and friends: Is this "vanity"? If it is, I stand for it.

27.

Bhagat Singh's Last Petition

To

The Punjab Governor

Sir,

With due respect we beg to bring to your kind notice the following:

That we were sentenced to death on 7th October 1930 by a British Court, L.C.C Tribunal, constituted under the Sp. Lahore Conspiracy Case Ordinance, promulgated by the H.E. The Viceroy, the Head of the British Government of India, and that the main charge against us was that of having waged war against H.M. King George, the King of England.

The above-mentioned finding of the Court pre-supposed two things:

Firstly, that there exists a state of war between the British Nation and the Indian Nation and, secondly, that we had actually participated in that war and were therefore war prisoners.

The second pre-supposition seems to be a little bit flattering, but nevertheless it is too tempting to resist the desire of acquiescing in it.

As regards the first, we are constrained to go into some detail. Apparently there seems to be no such war as the phrase indicates. Nevertheless, please allow us to accept the validity of the pre-supposition taking it at its face value. But in order to be correctly understood we must explain it further. Let us declare that the state of war does exist and shall exist so long as the Indian toiling masses and the natural resources are being exploited by a handful of parasites. They may be purely British Capitalist or mixed British and Indian or even purely Indian. They may be carrying on their insidious exploitation through mixed or even on purely Indian bureaucratic apparatus. All these things make no difference.

No matter, if your Government tries and succeeds in winning over the leaders of the upper strata of the Indian Society through petty concessions and compromises and thereby cause a temporary demoralization in the main body of the forces. No matter, if once again the vanguard of the Indian movement, the Revolutionary Party, finds itself deserted in the thick of the war. No matter if the leaders to whom personally we are much indebted for the sympathy and feelings they expressed for us, but nevertheless we cannot overlook the fact that they did become so callous as to ignore and not to make a mention in the peace negotiation of even the homeless, friendless and penniless of female workers who are alleged to be belonging to the vanguard and whom the leaders consider to be enemies of their utopian non-violent cult which has already become a thing of the past; the heroines who had ungrudgingly sacrificed or offered for sacrifice their husbands, brothers, and all that were nearest and dearest to them, including themselves, whom your government has declared to be outlaws. No matter, it your agents stoop so low as to fabricate baseless calumnies against their spotless characters to damage their and their party's reputation. The war shall continue.

It may assume different shapes at different times. It may become now open, now hidden, now purely agitational, now fierce life and death struggle. The choice of the course, whether bloody or comparatively peaceful, which it should adopt rests with you. Choose whichever you like. But that war shall be incessantly waged without taking into consideration the petty (illegible) and the meaningless ethical ideologies. It shall be waged ever with new vigour, greater audacity and unflinching determination till the Socialist Republic is established and the present social order is completely replaced by a new social order, based on social prosperity and thus every sort of exploitation is put an end to and the humanity is ushered into the era of genuine and permanent peace. In the very near future the final battle shall be fought and final settlement arrived at.

The days of capitalist and imperialist exploitation are numbered. The war neither began with us nor is it going to end with our lives. It is the inevitable consequence of the historic events and the existing environments. Our humble sacrifices shall be only a link in the chain that has very accurately been beautified by the unparalleled sacrifice of Mr. Das and most tragic but noblest sacrifice of Comrade Bhagawati Charan and the glorious death of our dear warrior Azad.

As to the question of our fates, please allow us to say that when you have decided to put us to death, you will certainly do it. You have got the power in your hands and the power is the greatest justification in this world. We know that the maxim "Might is right" serves as your guiding motto. The whole of our trial was just a proof of that. We wanted to point out that according to the verdict of your court we had waged war and were therefore war prisoners. And we claim to be treated as such, i.e., we claim to be shot dead instead of to be hanged. It rests with you to prove that you really meant what your court has said.

We request and hope that you will very kindly order the military department to send its detachment to perform our execution.

Yours,

BHAGAT SINGH

Shadman Chowk in Lahore, the spot where Bhagat Singh, Rajguru and Sukhdev were hanged in 1931.

The Tribune.

LAHORE, WEDNESDAY, MARCH 25, 1931.

BHAGAT SINGH, RAJGURU AND SUKHDEV EXECUTED.

NO "LAST INTERVIEW" WITH RELATIONS.

Shouts Emerge From Jail.

Removed to Distant Place.

Thick Veil of Secrecy.

Bhagat Singh's Letter

The Tribune's front page on March 25, 1931 after the execution of Bhagat Singh, Rajguru and Sukhdev.

Ajit Singh
Bhagat Singh's uncle

Swaran Singh
Bhagat Singh's uncle

Vidyavati
Bhagat Singh's mother

Shukhdev Thapar
(15 May 1907 – 23 Mar. 1931)

Shivaram Rajguru
(24 Aug.1908 – 23 Mar. 1931)

Batukeshwar Dutt
(18 Nov. 1910 – 20 July 1965)